GOD'S SPIRITUAL WARRIOR'S DAILY PRAYER HANDBOOK

52 WEEKS OF SOUL-EMPOWERING PRAYERS THAT STRENGTHEN YOUR ARMOR FOR BEGINNERS AND ADVANCED YOUNG CHRISTIANS AND CHRISTIAN WARRIORS

DR. ROCKY SPENCER

CONTENTS

A SPECIAL GIFT TO THE READER !!

Included with your purchase of this book is our God's Spiritual Warriors Checklist.

In this checklist you will receive the 5 steps necessary to prepare for being a Spiritual Warriors. It will fortify you with the right tools, environment, and other techniques needed to get the most benefit out of your Handbooks.

Click below and let us know which email to deliver to.

drrockyspencer.com

INTRODUCTION

My Dear Brothers and Sisters,

I am so excited for you to take this journey of faith and deepen your relationship with our Lord and Savior. Over these next 52 weeks, you will be challenged to deepen your prayer life and spend significant time with God. These prayers are meant to help you surrender your will and fully accept His. We cannot be good soldiers unless we are following the direction of our General. He is our Commander, and we are here to do what He commands us.

This book works as a companion to the *God's Spiritual Warriors Devotional Handbook*, so if you have not already, I encourage you to also purchase that book so you can work through the handbooks concurrently. Consider the next year to be a training period as you do spiritual lifting to become a warrior. God has called you out of darkness into his glorious light, but you still have some heavy lifting to do. Make sure that you are in the Word each day and spending time in His marvelous presence.

I pray that God's blessing pour out on you and you journey through this time with Him.

Sincerely,

Dr. Rocky Spencer

1

JANUARY - ANXIETY

WEEK 1

*D*ear God,

   I fully admit that I have been carrying around anxiety that I have not surrendered to you. I know that you love me and you want what is best for me. I know that you will take away these feelings or correct my situation if only I ask. Father, please move me out of my own way and allow me to accept your comfort and your peace.

I have been carrying around this weight with me for so long. I am exhausted. I want to experience your joy and your peace again. I want to be still and know that you are in control of my life. Yet, when I begin to feel overwhelmed by the stressors of life, I treat you as a last resort. I look around to every source except for the source of my life. Forgive me for my pride and my unwillingness to surrender to you. When I am anxious and concerned, help me to turn to you first.

Help me remember that you have not given me an anxious spirit. By your mere presence, I am able to be strong and courageous. You have given yourself to me so that I may be emboldened in your spirit, and I may feel your presence at all times. I am blessed and honored to have a piece of you that even the Israelites did not have—your Holy Spirit. You continually bless me and uplift me, helping me to soar when I do not even have the confidence to walk.

Remind me daily that your plan is better than mine, and your ways are higher than mine. Help me remember that you have created a future for me that is meant to help me and not to harm me. You are constantly working things out for my good, and you are behind the scenes of every situation. I cannot even fathom the work of your hands! I can never understand how you would love me so much that you would want to work through the details of my life. Yet, every day, you are encouraging me to grow stronger in my faith and accept disappointment as a sign that what I wanted was not nearly as good as what you have for me.

Please never let me become downcast when I do not meet the expectations of others. Help me to remember that I am blessed when I am persecuted for doing good. What the world despises, you love. Every time I feel that I am not good enough, you are there to remind me that I am more than enough because you made me.

Father, I know that the next year will be full of ups and downs. There will be moments when my anxiety is great within me, and there will be moments when my flesh fails. The future can be terrifying, and it is so easy to let my mind get ahead of me. But God, you already know the future, and you have already ordered my steps. I do not need to be anxious; I simply have to continue to stay in the center of your will. I will never be perfect, but you do not expect me to be. You simply ask that I show up and work on our relationship every single day. You will sustain me and you will give me the confidence to keep striving.

Please make the person you want me to be.

Amen.

WEEK 2

Dear God,

I am so grateful for everything you have done in my life. I deserve none of it. I am not worthy at all, and still you have called me your child. As my Father, you only desire what is best for me, and I can have the confidence that you are in charge of my future. What a stark difference it is to have that confidence. What a beautiful change to not have to fear or worry.

Father, as I sit and reflect on the last few months, I am reminded that anxiety has no place in my life. You have written me a prescription for something that is even better than an antidepressant. Your perfect peace falls on me when my anxiety threatens to overwhelm me. You have invited me into a relationship with you where I am constantly reminded that there is nothing that you cannot do. You become my strength is the midst of my weakness.

Where can I go apart from your presence? Psalm 139 reminds me that even in the depths of my despair, you are with me (NIV). You formed me in my mother's womb and there is nothing you do not know about me. You are aware of every worry and anxiety I carry. You knew what burdens I would bear before I was even born. You gave me the choice of laying those burdens on you or continuing to carry them on my own.

God, help me to lay those burdens down. You are calling me to a spirit of levity and joy. I cannot fully accept your peace if I am constantly going back to my anxieties and fretting over my future. You told me to come to you because your yoke is easy and your burden is light. Release me from my fear and anxiety and let me bask in your presence.

On the other hand, Lord, you might be calling me to endure this season so that I may grow to rely on you more fully. Like Paul experiencing the thorn in his side, I may have to deal with this anxiety so that you can be glorified. If that is your will, let me boast in my deficiencies because you are giving me strength. The anxiety and worry that has taken me captive might be a tool to draw me closer to you.

However you use this anxiety in my life, help me to fully surrender to your will. Though I have my own ideas of how I want the situation to play out, I know that it is more important to listen to what you have to say and give up my desires for your plan. That is a difficult reality for me, but I want to fully embrace all you have for me in this life. I know that I will never be able to do that if I am trying to force you to answer my prayers in a way that pleases me. Lord, may your will be done in my life and may I glorify you no matter what the end result is.

Amen.

WEEK 3

Dear God,

I want to seek you with my whole heart, but it is difficult sometimes. The world is so loud, and it is so easy to be anxious when everything is shouting at me that I am not good enough. I often feel that I am a massive failure and that everyone would know it. I worry that people only put up with me to be nice. Late at night, I stay awake with fears about what other people think about me. I replay every single one of my mistakes and I am filled with embarrassment. How could anyone love someone like me? Thank you for loving someone like me.

Over the last year, I have had no hope to cling to apart from you. Thank you for always showing up and providing what I needed. What an awesome God you are to care for us so much when we continually disappoint and betray you. Even when I think of how easy it is to fall into my sin, I get anxious. I want to please you, but so often the pull of my fleshly desires is too much to handle. It overwhelms me.

Then I remember that Jesus was tempted while he was on our Earth. You reminded us in your Word that he experienced every temptation that is common to human beings. Yet, he was perfect and did not commit sin. Though he had the great advantage of being fully God and fully man, I know that does not mean that temptation never hit Him the same way it hits me. In his last days on Earth, He could have chosen not to go through with the terrible pain He was about to suffer. He could have let his anxiety get the best of Him and run away from the great burden He had to carry.

The fact that He did not run encourages me to stay strong in the midst of my trials. As you were there for Him in the Garden of Gethsemane, then again on the cross, you are here for me. How great is your love and how incredible is your grace. I do not need to be anxious about the future or worry about stumbling. You will be there to catch me when I fall and encourage me to get back up.

I do not deserve your grace. I cannot possibly merit your favor. The beauty is, though, that you do not expect me to. You pour it onto me freely, and you give me more grace each and every morning. Let me bask in your glory and relieve the tension in my mind. Each morning, may I rise and thank you for giving me another day of life. May I take assurance in the fact that my steps are already ordered. Help me to stay in the center of your will so that I can continue to please you. Help me to let go of my need for perfection because you do not require that from me. You just require me to show up and love you more each day.

You are my peace, Lord.

Amen.

WEEK 4

Dear God,

I am so grateful and blessed that you love me enough to provide for my every need. When I am sad, you bring me comfort. When I am weary, you give me rest. You do not have to take care of me, but you do every single day. Who am I that you should be mindful of me? I am overwhelmed by your love. Unlike my anxiety, though, when your love overwhelms me, I feel perfect joy. I wake up in the morning with a smile on my face, and I go to bed praising you for everything you have done for me throughout the day.

You care for me as a mother cares for her newborn child. You surround me on all sides and protect me from all evil. You encourage me as I learn how to walk in your will, then start to run and jump and shout for joy. I know that I will never be perfect, and I know there will be times when I fall. I know in those moments, though, that you will not hold a grudge against me. I need only ask for forgiveness and you will lavish it onto me as a parent to a child.

Sometimes I worry about things that are out of my control. I worry about having enough money to spend or enough food to eat. I worry about the state of the world and the constant political and racial unrest. Getting on an airplane or even going to the grocery store fills me with unspeakable dread. Could this be the place where my life ends? Will my plane crash or will a shooter choose this story to end innocent lives? The world is filled with danger and uncertainty.

Then you tell me to take safety in the fact that you have overcome the world. You tell me not to worry about what I will wear or what I will eat because you care for all of your creatures. You keep your eye on the sparrow, so I can rest assured that you are also caring for me. Even if I were to lose my home and all my possessions, I would know that you have a plan and purpose for me. Even then you would uplift and encourage me. You would keep me safe from harm and teach me more and more to rely on your Spirit.

You are an awesome God. You give me an abundant life when the enemy is trying to destroy me. You take care of my needs to the point that I do not even need to worry what will happen tomorrow. You have already taken care of tomorrow and every day in the future. I continually praise you because of your goodness and mercy. Thank you so much for who you are and how you work out every anxious and stressful situation for my good. Thank you for loving me enough to even care how I am feeling at all. I love you so much.

Amen.

WEEK 5

Dear God,

Sorrow once filled my soul. Anxiety threatened to overwhelm me. Panic rose within me, and I was sure I was going to die, but there you were to calm my mind. In that moment, your peace washed over me and I could not comprehend how I could suddenly feel so calm and completely forget about my anxieties.

With your Spirit within me, I felt that I could melt into the floor. I was so relaxed and so at ease. Every concern that had been eating away at my thoughts and causing me unimaginable stress went away in the light of your perfect peace. My joy was restored, and I finally had the headspace to worship you and acknowledge your presence.

I understand, though, that not every moment in my life can be like that. There will be mountain experiences and valley experiences. One day I may shout from the rooftops that my God is with me; the next I may be huddled in my bed hiding from the world. Part of my humanity is dealing with the intense mental health problems that can overtake me. Even when I am hiding in bed, though, you are there with me. You are surrounding me with your love and holding me close to your heart. You speak words of comfort into my soul and assure me that everything will be okay.

I know that I can trust what you say, even if I am not ready to hear it in the moment. You are preparing my future even as I speak. You have poured out your Spirit onto me so that there will not be any situation I cannot handle. In your power, I know that there is nothing I cannot do. When anxiety overwhelms me, you will encourage me and strengthen my spirit. When I worry about tomorrow, you have already laid out every step. There is no detail, big or small, that you will not handle. I can fully surrender to your will knowing that your plan for me is perfect. Though I am not perfect and I will make many mistakes, you do not expect me to be blameless. You release me from the anxiety of perfectionism and love me exactly as I am.

As this first month of the year draws to a close, I have many questions and concerns. This year has unlimited potential and it might be the best year of my life or my worst. It may just be another forgettable year that goes by without much fanfare. I may lose my job, my home, or loved ones. Then again, I might gain all of these things afresh. It is easy to imagine worst case scenarios as I survey the enormity of the next 11 months, but you do not want that for me. You want me to experience your perfect peace and totally trust your promises. Whatever it is you want for me, help me to become exactly who you want me to be this year.

Amen.

2

FEBRUARY - LONELINESS

WEEK 1

*D*ear God,

You have seen my loneliness over the last few months, and you know how desperately I desire to have a companion in life. Whether that is a spouse or a spiritual mentor, I pray that you will send someone in my life who continues to pour into me your Word but also keeps me accountable to my relationship with you. I long to have a partner who can be there for me when my loneliness is overpowering me.

Yet I know that there is no person on this Earth who can provide the level of companionship that you can. I can be in a room with your greatest spiritual warriors and still feel that I am totally alone. With you, though, I know I am never alone. Unfortunately, there are moments when I fail to see that. There are dark moments when I think of every sin that has ever been committed against me and every heartbreak that has come my way. In those moments, I feel isolated and unworthy of love. Anger also stirs in my heart, and I question if your people are worthy of *my* love.

Please forgive me for not loving your people the way I should. Forgive me for not loving myself the way I should. You created me with a purpose, and part of that purpose is to love others as I love myself. Sometimes I have a hard time loving others or I have a hard time accepting other people's love for me. I know this is the main reason that I feel so alone. I am causing my own stumbling block.

Help me to fellowship with other believers in a healthy and uplifting way. Allow me to grow in companionship and concern with members of my church community. Let our friendships be like that of Paul and Timothy, or Jesus' disciples. Help me to build positive relationships with my co-workers and give me words to say that show them your love. Let those relationships grow like Paul, Priscilla, and Aquila. May I use every relationship in my life to glorify you and display your great love.

I know that I am not alone and you have not created me to be so. Even when I am feeling like the last person on this planet, remind me to get out of my bubble and love on your people. By showing your love to others, I will be reminded that loneliness does not have to have a foothold in my life. Thank you for creating me with a purpose and a passion to show love to your children.

Father, let this month especially be a time when I can fellowship with other believers and spend time worshipping you in a community setting. Though I know that is not a requirement for my relationship with you, it is so uplifting to be surrounded by others who love you. I know that even if only two or three are gathered, you will also be there. Allow us to sharpen each other, as iron sharpens iron, and meditate on your Word. Let all of our interactions be fruitful and glorify you.

In your Holy and Precious name I pray,

Amen.

WEEK 2

Dear God,

In all the times I have felt alone and abandoned, I was able to cling to the assurance that you were always with me and would never leave me. I know that I am never truly alone because the creator of the universe dwells with me. You are present in every affliction, every anxiety, and every heartache. You have spoken the words that you will never leave me, nor forsake me. Your mighty hand keeps me from harm.

Unfortunately, there are times when I do not feel your presence or my negative self-talk keeps me from experiencing you fully. I know, Lord, that you are always close to me. If I feel any distance in our relationship, it is because I have moved away from you and am unwilling to draw near to you. Sometimes that is because I am in the midst of sin and I am too ashamed to come into your presence. Other times, it is because I have filled my schedule with things that do not honor you, and I do not make our relationship a priority.

In those moments, I feel the deepest loneliness. Being outside of your presence makes me feel lost and untethered to anything. I feel like a piece of my heart is missing. God, I can only imagine what I would feel like if I had no relationship. What would it be like if I had to spend an eternity without you? Hell can contain no punishment worse than feeling far away from you.

I praise you that you have rescued me from the inevitability of that eternal separation. When you sent Jesus to die on the cross for us, you eliminated the distance between us. You desire a deep relationship with me, and you desire my affection and time in return. There is no need you do not address in my life and no problem you cannot fix. The depths of your love for me are endless.

You have never left me, even when I never deserved it. You drew near to me in the times that I needed you the most. Even when I pushed you away, you stayed right where you were and waited for me to come to my senses. When I screamed and shouted and tried to force you out of my life, you just stood there and took it. Afterward, you forgave me and let me know that I was loved by you. I truly do not deserve the grace and love you constantly bestow upon me.

All of your children are so blessed to experience your presence. We understand that we could have been without you for all of eternity. You could have left us alone without any hope or chance for salvation. Every other false god and idol does that to its worshippers. When Elijah challenged the prophets of Baal on Mt. Carmel, they screamed and shouted and danced around until they bled, and nobody showed up for them. How lonely it must be to worship a false god. You showed up on that mountain after a simple prayer, and you consumed the altar in fire.

We trust that you are with us, and because of that we know that we do not need to feel alone in your presence. You give us everything we need, and when our lives come to an end, we will be with you forever in glory. That is the greatest relationship we could ever hope for. We are so grateful for your boundless love and companionship.

Amen.

WEEK 3

Dear God,

I think about the loneliness I experience sometimes, and I get worried about the future. Anxiety fills me and tells me that I will always feel this sense of dread and loneliness. It tells me that I could be in a room full of people and they all hate me and will reject me. Even when I am with other people, I feel out of place and unwanted. Even when everyone is being kind to me, there is a voice inside telling me that they are all lying, that they do not really want me around. Such deep feelings of isolation surround me. Nowhere feels like the place I belong, and my heart is getting tired.

The depths of my despair in those moments knows no bounds. The fear of being alone, of dying alone, makes it hard to function. All I can do in those moments is pray. That is what you want from me. You want me to pray when I am lonely. You want me to draw near to your presence and bask in your company. I am grateful that you have given your time and attention to me. Still, I feel that I need someone next to me: someone I can see and touch and talk with.

The thought of being alone in the future terrifies me. The anxiety of going through more historic and traumatic events in the future without someone by my side is too much for me to bear. Just like Adam, I need a companion to experience life with. I need a partner in life and in ministry. Help my companion to complement my strengths and help me to complement theirs. Give us a holy union that no man can break apart. Help us to both be the people we need to be in you.

At the same time, though, I do not want anyone in my life who is not meant to be there. Being with someone who is wrong for me can be just as lonely as not having anyone at all. I need wisdom and discernment to know who should be in my life and who needs to go. I want all of my relationships to be God honoring and fruitful for your Kingdom. If someone is getting in the way of my spiritual journey, remove them from my life.

I know that like Abraham, I will have to climb the mountain of faith on my own. There will be people that I have to leave behind so that I can get closer to you and follow in obedience. While I do not like the idea of having less people in my life, I know that it is more important to let you prune the branches that need to be pruned. Some people just cannot be part of my future, and I need to learn to be okay with that.

God, above all things, help me to glorify you. In all of my relationships, let me remain steadfast to your Word. Allow me the wisdom to let go of any negative relationships, but also restore my heart when they are gone. It is never easy saying goodbye to someone, even if it is your will. Even so, I know that you will be there to take care of me when the sadness of broken relationships overwhelms me. I also know that you will bring better relationships into my life, and for that I praise you endlessly.

Amen.

WEEK 4

Dear God,

Jesus told us that the greatest commandment was to love you with our whole heart, mind, and spirit. The second greatest command was to love others as I love myself. It is so easy for me to love other believers as myself, but I often struggle to show the same level of love and care for those who do not believe in you. Often, I purposely isolate myself from nonbelievers, falsely believing that being around them could cause my faith to weaken.

When I make those decisions, I end up breaking your heart and making myself even more lonely. Sometimes nonbelievers are the only people around. By choosing to discriminate against them and not engage in meaningful conversations, it is like I am telling you that they are not important to me. It is almost like I am saying I would prefer they spend eternity apart from you.

I know that I cannot evangelize to every person I meet, but I usually do not try to speak your name to anyone. I consider any separation from you to be extremely difficult, yet I never try to show my love for you to them. God, I know that other people are experiencing that deep and dark loneliness of being outside of your presence, and I am doing nothing to draw them closer to you. Forgive me for my lack of concern or compassion. May you put the desire of my heart to always take care of your people and use your words to rescue them from their intense loneliness.

Father, as your servant, I know it is my responsibility to be your hands and feet. You want me to go to reach as many people as I can to declare your grace and greatness. You want me to get down in the gutters with the lowest of humanity and tell them of your merciful love. More importantly, you want me to *show* that love.

Help me to be more loving to everyone, Lord. Help me to love my neighbor as myself, or even better than I love myself. I want to be an example of who you are, and I definitely cannot be that example if I am not displaying your love. Increase in me the capacity to love and forgive. Give me compassion for those who need it the most and deserve it the least. Break my heart for what breaks yours and help me to love who you love.

If I ever fail you in this way or cause your people harm, grant me your grace. It is not my desire to hurt anyone intentionally, and I do not want to cause anyone to feel deep loneliness. So many people in the world are hurting, and you can use me as a light in the darkness. You can make me a beacon of hope and friendship. As a moth is drawn to a flame, let the lonely and downtrodden be drawn to the amount of you that they see in me.

Help me to comfort your children the way you have so graciously comforted me. Even when they irritate me or push me away, let me be as persistent as you are. Allow me the patience and understanding to accept people as they are, as you accept us so willingly. Keep me encouraged as I try to help your people, and do not let me give up on helping when the going gets tough. Father, I sincerely desire to be your witness. Thank you for giving me this desire, and thank you for assuring me of your presence. I know that I am never alone, and I can bring that same peace to others because of your Spirit. You are an awesome God.

Amen.

3

MARCH - FAITH

WEEK 1

*D*ear God,

You know that I am terrified of the dark. When the lights are off, I immediately go to the worst-case scenario. I imagine unseen creatures lurking around or prowlers breaking in with the intent to murder me. Darkness does not necessarily bring such bad luck, but it brings me uncertainty. I can no longer see the scope of a room, and my lack of sight causes me to doubt my safety.

Faith feels like that to me sometimes. When I know your plan and know that I am following your will, I am assured that everything is going to be okay. When the "lights" go off, though, and you ask me to trust in what I cannot see, I immediately become apprehensive. Though you can see and know all things, I sometimes doubt my safety around you. When you call me to put my faith totally in you and follow you into the unknown, I feel that familiar weight of fear and anxiety, even though I know you do not want me to walk in anxiety. You have said to me, "Be anxious for nothing, but in everything by prayer and supplication with thanksgiving, let your requests be made known unto God" (Philippians 4:6-7, NIV). "Fear not" is actually in the Bible 365 times! That is one per day! I guess you really mean what you say!

Forgive me for my lack of faith in you. If I cannot trust in what I do not see or understand, I should at least be able to trust in the many times you have proven your promises to be true. I can look back through my life and see every instance where you asked me to step out in blind faith and the situation worked for my good. I have praised you for those circumstances. I have testified about them. The high of experiencing your miracles makes me think I will never doubt in you again. Then you ask me to put on a blindfold and go base jumping, and suddenly I forget my proclamation to trust you in all things.

Help me to hold fast to Proverbs 3:5-6: "Trust in the Lord with all thine heart and lean not unto thine own understanding. In all thy ways acknowledge Him and He will direct thy paths" (NIV). Also, I cling to Ephesians 5:8, which says, "For you were once in darkness but now you are in light in the Lord. Walk as

Children of the Light" (NIV). Help me to walk in that way, Father.

Father, I know that whatever you are calling me to in life is in accordance to your perfect plan. I am assured that you only put me in situations that grow me close to you. Believing in what I know is easy. Believing in what I do not know is horrible. Still, I ask you to increase my faith. Please keep placing me in situations where I have to put my faith in you and you alone. Like Isaiah, let me declare, "Here I am, Lord, send me!" Even though I have no idea what the future holds and what creatures lurk in the dark, I want to totally rely on you.

Amen.

WEEK 2

Dear God,

One thing that I am absolutely sure about is that you sent your son to die for my sins, and on the third day he rose from the grave and defeated death and sin forever. This is something I believe wholeheartedly without a stitch of empirical evidence or historical data. It is the cornerstone of my faith in you.

Every day, though, I am faced with people who doubt your very existence. They tell me I am foolish for blindly believing in a book written 2,000 years ago. They challenge my belief system and ask me to back up my claims about your presence in my life. When all I have to offer is my personal testimony of your grace, they tell me that my argument is weak and I am nothing but a sheep.

O Lord, how lucky I am to be a sheep in your flock. Even when I am faced with the severe doubt from so many nonbelievers, I thank you that I am firm in my beliefs about your sacrifice. I thank you that I am too dumb to doubt your grace. I thank you for being my Shepherd and leading me where you want me to go, even to those dark and scary places we talked about last week.

I thank you that I can turn to you at all times. That when Christ was sacrificed, a direct line of communication was established between you and me. When the veil was torn, your presence landed on humanity in a way that it never had before. God, you are so incredible to love us so much.

In Christ alone my hope is found. My faith is firm on the rock of His salvation. I will not put my faith anywhere else because other entities will fail me. In no one but you can I find the confidence to hope and believe fully. Every word you say is true. Every promise you make comes to pass. My faith is strong in you because you have shown me that you are trustworthy and faithful to me. You have demonstrated your love in a way that no one else could do. You supply my every need, even when I feel panicked about the future.

Above all, I have faith that Jesus Christ went to the cross and bore my sins. I have faith that He rose from the grave on the third day. That faith is almost childlike. I do not have to see or have proof that it happened. When I was told about Jesus, I believed in my heart and never had to question it. I praise you Lord for allowing me to experience such blind faith. It is an honor for me to be counted as one of your children. I thank you for the person who first told me about your sacrifice. I thank you for how your Spirit came upon me and showed me the way to salvation. I thank you for your Living Word that, though written centuries ago, is still relevant today. You are as real now as you were then, and I am excited that I get to put my faith in him who is worthy to be praised.

Amen.

WEEK 3

Dear God,

I know that my faith will not improve without a certain amount of doubt. Whether that doubt rises from my own concerns or it comes from the naysayers who do not believe in you, I know that doubt will cause me to trust more. Thomas the disciple often comes to mind for me. He did not believe that Jesus had really been resurrected until he put his fingers in the holes of the wounds. Sometimes, I think Thomas gets a bad reputation because of that instance. You can handle our doubts, and you have answers to all of our questions.

I do know, though, that in order to go deeper in my faith, I am going to have to endure tests and trials in my life. Only by having these experiences will I be able to expand and increase my faith. It is hard and awkward to ask you to make certain aspects of my life more difficult. Honestly, I would prefer it if you could make my life easier and keep me from all manners of negativity. I prefer my comfort zone of belief without challenges, but it is in those challenges that I become strong. That I develop my personal muscles.

You want a better life for me. You want me to experience the depths of your love by experiencing the bitterness of the world's hate. You want me to be assured of my faith by sending people and obstacles in my way that would get me to try and doubt you. In my spiritual warfare, I will slay each one of these doubts.

I will arm myself with your Breastplate of Righteousness, your Belt of Truth, the Shoes of your Gospel of Peace, the Shield of Faith, the Helmet of Salvation, and the Sword of the Spirit—which is the Word of God! I will not try to arm myself with man's armor—education, reasoning, philosophy, wealth, or power. They would be for me like little David trying to wear the all too heavy Hebrew armor to stand against Goliath. I must trust in the spiritual armor that you have provided. I do not dare go up against doubt with my own defenses. Did not even Jesus have his faith challenged by Satan in the wilderness? He came through it by rebuking Satan with the Word of God and by speaking out loud to the doubts. May I trust the one who has already been there where I often am and has come out victorious. The Scripture tells me that he was tempted in every way that I am tempted, and yet did not sin.

A caterpillar only emerges to be a beautiful butterfly through the struggles in the cocoon. It is that day to day struggle that builds those wings and ultimately sets the young butterfly free to soar. Were it to be released from the struggle, it would never develop and its life would be short and pitiful. Set me free to soar, Father! Through every spiritual struggle and battle, let me develop those beautiful wings!

Amen.

WEEK 4

Dear God,

Today I stand in boldness declaring that what you have promised to me has already come to pass. I know that to you, a single day is like a thousand years for me. You have already looked down upon my life and have seen how every situation would work out. When I prayed to you for answers to my problems, you had the solution ready to go. Even before I knew I had a problem, you saw the way out for me.

That is how I know that your promises are true. Even when I do not know the problem yet, you know the answer. So I can claim in faith that your promises are mine. Even if I have to wait 10 or 15 years to see the fruition of those promises, I believe that you have already poured them out upon me. When they come to pass, I will have no doubt that it was you who put them in my path. I will not believe the false narrative that I received good things because I was patient and "the universe" rewarded me. No, as a believer in your promises, I know that every good and perfect thing comes from you.

James 1:17 says that, "Every good gift and every perfect gift is from above, and comes down from the Father of lights with whom there is no variation or shadow of turning." And you, Father, love to lavish your gifts upon us. Jesus told us in Matthew 7:11, "If you being evil know how to give good gifts to your children, how much more will your Father who is in heaven give good things to those who ask him." A third verse I lean on is Psalm 37:4, which says, "Delight yourself also in the Lord and he will give you the desires of your heart" (NIV). What a promise that is! And yet, it is not a blank check for everything I want. It is clear that the desires of my heart are somehow linked to my delighting myself in you. When I truly take delight in you, Lord—enjoy your presence, seek your guidance, and sit at your feet, then those desires that fill my heart are truly put there by you. Since you put them there, you will absolutely fulfill those desires in me. That is so exciting to know and be able to trust!

So help me to develop the patience to wait—to wait for all of the wonderful gifts that you are going to bestow on me! Help me to wait for my desires to grow in harmony with your will for my life. Help me to never lose sight of just how much you love me and want to bestow on me the desires of my heart. Most of all, Lord, help me to have the faith that those promises are mine. Life will try to get in the way of our relationship. The world will try to make me doubt that what you say is for me. Even other Christians will tell me that what I believe is not true. They will put you in a box that you would never exist in and say that you do not operate outside of that box. If that advice comes from trusted mentors and spiritual advisors, I will be tempted to listen to them rather than you.

Increase my faith and boldness to believe in what you have promised me. Do not let me be discouraged by the words of other believers. I know that only you are worthy of my unyielding faith. Because of that, I will believe in what you have for me without questioning you. Yes, today I stand in boldness declaring that what you have promised to me has already come to pass!

Amen.

WEEK 5

Dear God,

What I know about soldiers is that they are strong, both physically and mentally. They are able to withstand an enormous amount of pressure and are willing to enter the worst situations. They are disciplined and obedient. Father, I want my faith to be as strong as a soldier. Even if I am physically weak, I want my faith in you to be strong. If my faith was represented by a human being, I would want it to be a bodybuilder. I would lift weights every day and eat an enormous amount of carbs to bulk up. I would be focused and disciplined.

It helps me to think of my faith in this way because it helps me to see what I need to do personally to strengthen it. If I let my faith sit untrained, it will continue to be weak and useless. If I never exercise it, or outright ignore it, it will be unable to support the weight of my concerns. Truthfully, though, I do not always know the best way to strengthen it. I am not an expert. You are, though. You know exactly how to train me so that my faith in you becomes as strong as Samson, as obedient as Paul, and as brave as Daniel.

Lord, put my faith through boot camp and teach me how to rely on you completely. I want to learn how to be strong and courageous and to put my faith in you. When I am weak and the ground I stand on is shaking, I want to stand firm in the faith I have. Your word is a firm foundation, and I know that if I am planted and rooted in it, I will not be shaken. Though foes will try to destroy me and the enemy will beat down my door, I know I will be safe with you.

Amen.

4

APRIL - COMFORT

WEEK 1

*D*ear God,

You have witnessed every devastation and heartbreak I have ever had. You did not just witness them; you were right beside me throughout. When I cried out to you in the midst of my despair, you wrapped me in your loving arms and held on tight. When no one else was there for me, you supported me and nursed my heart. You restored your joy within me and gave me a new song to sing.

I have had my fair share of pain in life, but you have always been there. When the world was out of control, you were steadfast and true. When I could not even stand on my own two feet, you were my support. It makes no sense that you would want to be there for me, but your Word tells us that you are close to the brokenhearted. My heart has surely been broken many times. Even when I did not feel your presence with me, I knew it was there. I was able to look back after the fact and see how you had carried me through.

Even now it brings comfort to me to know that you are always there. I could cry with tears of joy at the immensity of your love. No one else has given me so much support throughout my life, nor have they stuck around for my darkest moments. In fact, as I reflect on those times, I can see that almost no one else was there. There were maybe one or two people, but there was always you.

You bring me joy, O Lord. You bring peace and prosperity. There is nothing that I have to worry about or fear because you will be there for every moment. Your constant presence gives me hope. The promise of your presence brings me encouragement. Like a security blanket, you comfort me in times of confusion. I am wrapped in your love, protected by your armor. No arrow will pierce it; no weight will crush it.

Your Word reminds me that though I may be pressed, I will not be crushed. Though I may be persecuted, you will never abandon me. Even if I am struck down, I will not be destroyed. Your joy will be my strength, and your help will be my comfort. Your loving words will be a balm for my soul, healing all wounds and uplifting my head.

Still, I know there will be times when I am tempted to look for comfort from other sources. The world will tell me that I should find my comfort there. It will provide so many attractive options to turn to for help. It would be so easy and convenient to turn to substances to numb my pain or to physical relationships to distract me from it. The enemy wants me to take my eyes off of you and seek out comfort and pleasure from the world. Even if he just gets me distracted and makes me doubt your ability to comfort me, he will be satisfied.

Do not let me stumble, Lord. Even if the Devil pursues me with all of his armies, provide a way out for me. I do not want to displease you, and I do not want to act in a way that I would regret later on. Help me to only seek comfort from you, to only accept it from you. I know that it is best when it comes from you, and it is the best healing. Remind me in times when it is so easy to take my eyes off of you. Bring peace to my soul, even when it makes no sense that I should have peace. I love you, Lord, and I am so appreciative of the comfort and healing you consistently bring me.

Amen.

WEEK 2

Dear God,

The world is such a discouraging place. Society constantly pressures us to do more and expect less. If we are not running ourselves ragged in the pursuit of financial or professional success, we are made to feel like failures. If we are not focused on having as many romantic encounters as possible, we are made to feel like we are unworthy of love. If we spend our time in pursuit of you and your glory, we are made to feel like overzealous religious freaks.

The world does not understand us, and they do not understand you. You warned your disciples of this. You told them that the world would hate them as it hated you. You prepared them for the harsh reality and cruelty this world brings. Still, it is hard not to feel hurt by how we are treated. We desire to be liked, even loved, by everyone. We seek the approval of others, and when they reject us, it feels like a personal attack on our character.

Following you is difficult. Being rejected by the world is painful. Even so, you are there to comfort us when we are in the midst of that rejection. You remind us that our pain has a purpose and our rewards will be found in Heaven. You caution us to be in the world, but not be of the world because that will separate us from you. It is almost a compliment if the world hates us. It shows that we are following you in the way we have been called to. It does not ease the hurt, though.

No, Lord, only you are able to do that. Only you bring us comfort and hope when we are sad and alone. Only you are there to remind us that you love us with an unconditional love that is bigger than all of the love combined. It is an unfailing love that does not abandon us in our time of greatest need. It is the same love that has carried me through so many dark moments in my life. It has surrounded me on all sides, and filled me with warmth.

There is no logical reason that rejection should be an encouragement to me. Being hated should not bring me pleasure. Yet I will boast in the world's disdain of me as long as it is pointing others to your cross. If my suffering is a testimony to your grace, then it has served a great purpose.

All I want to do is bring your children back to you. As I have been rescued from sin and death, I want to rescue others. The enemy does not want that to happen, and he will send obstacles in my way to try and defeat me. He will turn the hearts of men against me and try to plant seeds of doubt in my heart. He will do everything in his power to stop me from spreading your light. How comforted I will be by your presence in that moment, Lord. How grateful I will be for the promises you have given me. Every hardship will be a reminder of how much you love me and how much we are foiling the enemy's plan.

You are a good Father. Your joy fills my heart, and your peace calms my spirit. Your unfathomable love keeps me going in times of distress. Thank you for trials and tribulations, Lord, because they are a sign that I am living in the center of your will. Nothing brings me greater comfort than that.

Amen.

WEEK 3

Dear God,

I have mentioned many times how afraid I am of the future. Lord, I am so afraid. Then I read Jeremiah 29:11 over and over again. "For I know the plans I have for you," you say to us (NIV). Even though those words were originally meant to bring comfort to the Israelites, those words can still bring me comfort today. After all, you are the same God now that you were then. You have not changed. You will not change.

You still know the plans you have for us, and they are to help and not harm us. You are not actively creating situations where we feel discouraged. You do not lead us into the valley of the shadow of death, then expect us to find our way out all on our own. You are not cruel, and you do not intend for our destruction. The psalmist David says that even when he walks through the valley of the shadow of death, he will fear no evil because your rod and staff will comfort him. I want to be encouraged by the same promises. Though I have been through difficult moments, you have always been there to carry me through them. It would be foolish for me to continue to fear the future when you are already there. You have already ordained it.

You had a plan for the Israelites when you let them be carried into exile. You promised them that one day they would return to the land of their ancestors. You promised them that a savior would come and deliver them from their enemies. Though it took centuries, you fulfilled that promise. I am reminded once again that your timing is very different than ours, but it is perfect. If we had our way, we would likely end up miserable. You know the perfect plans for us and the perfect path for us to take. Even if we divert from the path, you create other roads to follow.

What a comfort it is to me that I cannot possibly mess up your plan for my life. You have already prepared for every possible choice I could make and every disobedient moment I have. You have planned for my temper tantrums and childish breakdowns. Even when I feel like I am in a desert place, you will lead me to my version of the Promised Land, as you did for the Israelites centuries before their exile into Babylon. You are like an ultimate puzzle master, putting every piece into place, then allowing us to feel clever when we look back and see what you have done in our lives.

It is a joy to follow your plan for our lives, O Lord. Staying in the center of your will brings us so much comfort. You surround us on all sides and fight out battles. You even ward off the things that are unseen. Even when it seems your will is taking me through the eye of a hurricane, I know that even there you will be with me. You will never leave me to my own devices, and I praise you wholeheartedly for that. Lord, I know that if you bring me to something, you will bring me through it. You brought the Israelites to the edge of the Red Sea. In front of them there was an uncrossable body of water, and behind them was the Egyptian army in hot pursuit. In that moment, Lord, you made a way where there was no way. You split the sea so that they could safely cross through it. When the Egyptians chased after them, you washed them away.

I take comfort in this: my future is in your hands, and you will always provide me a way when there is none.

Amen.

WEEK 4

Dear God,

Help me to comfort others. That is not always easy, Lord. Sometimes I feel awkward—what would I even say? Would the person I am comforting even want me there? If they were to reject my help during those times, I would feel stupid. My feelings would be hurt, and I would need someone to comfort me! What a risk it is to try and be present for people in their time of need.

Other times, I just would rather not come out of my comfort zone and reach out in case I say or do the wrong thing. I am prone to put my foot in my mouth. Too often words come out that neither make sense nor bring comfort. This is so not of you!

In 11 Corinthians 1:3-4, it says, "Blessed be the God and Father of our Lord Jesus Christ, the Father of mercies and God of all comfort, who comforts us in all our tribulation, that we may be able to comfort those who are in any trouble, with the comfort with which we ourselves are comforted by God" (NIV). You comfort me in my darkest times so that I can comfort those who are also in need of comfort.

You, my Father, never withhold your comfort from me. You are always there when I am hurt, discouraged, in pain. I feel your peace that passes all understanding, and I am comforted. You send people into my life at just the right time to bring me that comfort. Now you want me to take that comfort I have received and give it to those who suffer as well. Help me to be your arms of comfort to those around me who need to feel your comfort through human expression. Help me to dry tears, love unconditionally, and when words fail, help me to just be there to listen. Sometimes make me brave enough to sit in silence when no words are being spoken on either side.

Help me to comfort others even when it is inconvenient, when it brings up bad memories, when I do not feel well, and even when I do not even like or know the person who needs my comfort. Help me to comfort others. Not for how it will make me feel, but for how it will show your love to the person who needs it at that moment. May they see you in me as I comfort them.

My last request is the hardest. Help me to comfort my enemies. I know that my enemies are not yours. Most of them are your children. You prepare a place for them at your table, perhaps even right next to me. Soften my heart toward them. Help me to love them as I love myself. Humble my heart so that I am not offering them comfort out of vain conceit. It would be easy to see my enemy down and kick him where it hurts. That is definitely how the enemy would like me to respond. You want me to be like the Good Samaritan. You want me to take care of them to the best of my ability and assure them that everything will be okay. You want me to demonstrate Christ's love in a big way.

Allow me to be an ambassador of your comfort. Relieve me of any pride I may harbor, and fill my cup to overflowing so that the comfort I am giving is directly from you. As I often need a pat on the back or a kind word from someone, so do others. Help me to be "someone." Help me to be exactly what a hurting person needs at that time. Give me the words to say or the actions to take that would uplift their spirit. Move me out of my way and let me words and actions come from your Holy Spirit.

Amen.

5

MAY - GRACE

WEEK 1

*D*ear God,

When you sent your Son to die for us, you made a bridge between yourself and us. Before then, we were completely cut off from you and we were doomed to an eternity without you. It was only by the grace poured out after Christ's sacrifice that we were able to be saved. Oh, God, how did we favor such grace from you?

Thank you so much for this grace that you freely give us. Thank you for Jesus' sacrifice on the cross, and His willingness to suffer and die in our place. We were the ones who deserved death. It should have been us on the cross. It should have been me. Sometimes, I feel like I am constantly driving nails into Christ's hands and feet because I have such a hard time letting go of my sin. I want to honor you with my words and actions, but I get so caught up in what I want and desire.

When I think of the cross, I feel the depths of my sorrow and shame. I am keenly aware of my humanity and my inability to change apart from your grace. Help me to die daily to my sins and take up my cross. Help me to meditate on Christ's sacrifice more so that I may always be reminded what it cost for you to forgive my sins.

Pour out your grace onto me, but do not let me take it for granted. As Paul warned in Romans, I should not keep sinning so that I can receive more grace. Instead, I need to accept the grace that has been freely given, then with that grace I can flee from sin. Your grace empowers me to live a better lifestyle because I do not want to take advantage of your gift. I do not want to think of it as a get out of jail free card. It is not meant to be my excuse to do whatever I want.

Every day I experience your grace afresh, and it keeps me from stumbling. It helps me to stay upright when I think I am going to fall over and injure myself. It adds an extra cushion if I do happen to fall. Then it is there to encourage me to get right back up and pursue you again. When I want to wallow in my sin and shame, it is there telling me how much you love me, and how quickly you will forgive me. You will separate my sins as far as the east is from the west, and you will consider it no longer.

It makes no sense. We are the ones who commit sin, usually on a regular basis, but you were the one who paid for it. We will never be able pay back that loan, and we would be indebted to you forever. If you were cruel or evil, you would hold us to that debt and deny us of your love and attention until it was paid in full. Instead, you tell us that there is nothing for us to pay back. You also say that there is nothing we can do to earn it. It is truly a gift, and it is one that we must be willing to receive. God, I am willing to receive it. I am desperate to receive it. Thank you for this grace that is so freely given, and may I continually honor your gift.

Amen.

WEEK 2

Dear God,

I am so blown away by your abundant grace. I feel so unworthy for this great gift you have given to me. I have sinned, I have failed, and I have fallen time and time again. Yet, by the very definition of grace, you just keep forgiving, keep bringing me back to success, and keep picking me up. You did not die for me and give me this great gift to just let me squander it away. Your grace is not deserved, or even earned. Nothing I can do can buy me grace. In the Middle Ages, religious leaders sold indulgences to "forgive" people for their sins. Yet you do not require money. In fact, Jesus turned over tables when the Pharisees were taking bribes as sin offerings. He called them a "den of vipers." What a gift it is that we do not have to enter that den to be pardoned by you.

Some feel that they have to, by good works, earn their grace so that your favor will shine on them. You do not require that; you only receive it as an act of love and gratitude. You pour out your blessings of grace in abundance! I live in the light of your grace and receive it as warm sunshine on my face! As the seed of Adam, I do not surely deserve this grace. Romans 5:17 tells me that, "For if by one man's offence death reigned through the one, much more those who receive abundance of grace and of the gift of righteousness will reign in life through the One, Jesus

Christ" (NIV). The sacrifice of Jesus Christ was made that I may rise above the sin of Adam and enter into the Life of Christ.

Like a newborn baby, I have done nothing to deserve your lavish grace. A newborn baby can give nothing in return, cannot earn our love, keeps us up at night, and cries a lot! Still, we love that newborn baby and offer it grace for all of that just because of our great love for them. We hold them, comfort them, nourish them, wipe their tears, and fall in love with them over and over again. That is what you do for us. Your grace is undeserved yet freely given. Your grace is abundant no matter how far we stumble. It should make us dance with joy, proclaim it to everyone we meet, and live like we are forgiven. It should make us sleep peacefully knowing that all is well because of your grace.

My heart is overwhelmed just considering it. I could cry tears of joy when I consider your grace for me. I can get lost in the feeling of it. Like Mary considered your words and treasured them in her heart, I do the same with your grace. It covers me and propels me forward. If you gave us nothing else for the rest of eternity, your grace would be enough.

Help me to praise you ceaselessly. I know I have a tendency to take you for granted and act like I am somehow above worshipping you for what you have done. In those moments, bring me to my knees and remind me of every whip that Christ suffered and every nail that went into his hands. I never again want to act as if your grace is not the most important thing in my life. I want to demonstrate to others, through my words and actions, that your grace is transformative. I want people to witness the grace you have poured out in my life and desire to know more about it. I want your grace in me to be multiplied, then shared with others and multiplied in them as well.

Your grace will never run out, and for that we are so blessed. Let us drown in your grace, that we may only breathe in your presence.

Amen.

WEEK 3

Dear God,

If I could do it all on my own, if I accumulated great wealth, if I had the physical ability to win every race, then it would all be about me. Everyone would say, "Look at them! They are so powerful! They do not need anything, or anyone. They are amazing." It would be all about *me*. Oddly enough, though, when I am weak, when I am in doubt, when I have fallen or failed, then it is in those circumstances that your grace is magnified and made perfect, and I see the wonders of your grace.

So many times I have not had an answer to a particular problem. I wondered how I would get through. I have been down to my last dollar and suddenly, I have received an unexpected check in the mail. I have been worried about how I would afford food for the week when a generous friend or even stranger has blessed me financially. I have been stressed about a deadline, feeling deep dread and panic, when I have gotten an email that my time has been extended or I have finished with time to spare. None of these things happen because of anything that I have done but completely out of your grace.

I see that, without a doubt, your grace is made perfect in my weakness. I have seen so many mighty answers and so many instances where the only explanation could be that your grace has shown up and been made perfect in my life. I have been broken beyond recognition from a relationship when suddenly your grace shows up and my heart is mended, forgiveness is extended, and love is restored. I have survived pain and sickness through your grace and knew immediately that I was given the responsibility of sharing that grace with others; not because I willed myself to live, but because through your grace I had been given a second chance.

Your grace proves over and over that I have nothing to boast in myself. Nothing that is accomplished is done in my ability or will to pull myself up by the bootstraps. I am in no way the recipient of blessings because of anything I have done. If that were the case, then what would I need you for? What would be the point of your great sacrifice at Calvary? You died for my salvation because I could not earn it myself. In my weakness, you bring this wonderful grace that blesses me and amazes me and shows me that it is all you, not me.

God, let me boast in every weakness because in that weakness you will be glorified. Let me shout from the rooftops when I experience trials of any kind. I know that your grace will be right behind me to work out my situation. Your grace is sufficient for me, and for that I can only say "thank you."

Thank you that you are not like the world, who tells us that weakness is a flaw. Thank you that you do not berate us or make us feel worthless when we are at the end of ourselves. Thank you for not expecting perfection from us, or saying that you will only help those who would help themselves. Help us to let go of that false narrative, because we know from your Word that you will help anyone, even those who do not deserve it.

You constantly remind us of your presence in the midst of our struggles. You announce yourself and tell us to take heart. You are like a warrior who comes to fight for a helpless village when it is under siege. We certainly are helpless when we are left to our own devices, and we are even more so when we try to conquer sin without your presence. It is only by your grace that we are saved.

What joy fills my heart when I am faced with a challenge. What peace washes over me when my life feels like it is coming to an end. You will be there in every moment to lavish me in your grace and bestow upon me your strength. Let me never forget the sacrifice you made for me. Let me never believe that anything good in my life comes from a different source. You have given me everything I need by the power of your grace.

Amen.

WEEK 4

Dear God,

I want to be an instrument of your grace. I often fail at this because I am so human and so flawed. When people hurt me, I want to hurt them back. Rather than forgetting or turning the other cheek, I choose to carry anger and bitterness in my heart. Yet how can I accept your grace then turn around and deny it to others?

Jesus told us the story of the unforgiving servant in Matthew 28:21-35. The servant owed a great debt to his master, which the master forgave easily. Yet when another servant owed him a much smaller debt, he had that servant arrested. How often do I condemn people by the anger I show to them? How often do I show the wickedness of the enemy, rather than the beauty of your love? Unfortunately, it is likely much more often than I would want it to be. Even so, you do not hold that against me. That is the grace you show to me.

God, please increase grace in me so that I may show it more to others. I want to be a vessel of your grace, and be your mouthpiece to your children. Forgive me of my past sins and help me to repent toward anyone I have wronged. Going forward, help me to show grace to all of your people, especially those who do not deserve it. I know that I especially do not deserve it, and that has not stopped you from giving it to me.

Father, bring into my life people who need a touch of your grace. Bring into my path people who have been abandoned by the world, people who may have given up on themselves. Let me share with them the good news of your sacrifice and your grace. Put the words in my mouth to testify of your great works in my life and in the world as a whole. As you have taught me to comfort them, teach me to show grace to them.

Especially increase my grace toward those who have wronged me. I could write a 10-page list of every person that has hurt me in the past. I could go to every one of those people and demand their apologies. I could harass and belittle them, making them feel just as low as they once made me feel. Instead, I will burn the list and think of it no longer. I will show them kindness that they have never experienced, but not because I want to kill them with it. If my kindness and generosity flows out of petty feelings, it is not truly grace.

I do not want to disrespect the gift of your grace in that way. When I show grace to others, I want it to be pure and unselfish. I want to show grace to others as you have shown it to me; to forgive people without expecting them to admit to all of their wrongdoings toward me. Give me the grace to forgive freely and love deeply.

Amen.

6

JUNE - FEAR

WEEK 1

*D*ear God,

I have wasted so much of my life being afraid. I am afraid of my own shadow sometimes. Before I had you in my life, I feared death and what would happen to me in the afterlife. Since coming to know you, I have experienced your perfect love driving out all my fear. I know that I am constantly surrounded by you, and the largest armies of hell could not take me down. When you are for me, nothing can stand against me.

Father, your mercy gives me the confidence to boast in you. I no longer fear what is to the left or to the right. I know that you make my path straight and you guard me from my enemies.

69

Even if life should not go the way I hope or plan, my future is entirely in your hands. You have laid out the way for me, and I need only to walk through it.

I am honored and humbled that you would choose to fight for me. No king or world leader would ever stop to take care of his lowest constituent, but you are constantly taking care of me. I am a sinner, saved only by your grace. Apart from you, I am less than nothing. I am less important than a speck of dust. With you, I have boldness and assurance. I know I can walk with my head held high because my God is walking beside me.

Thank you, Lord, for protecting me on all sides. Thank you for keeping the enemies' arrows from piercing my skin. Even when I experience attacks, I know that you are protecting me from much worse. The world could do so much more to destroy me, but you are covering me.

I have nothing to fear because you are my protection and my strength. There is no one in Heaven or on Earth that is mightier than you. No forces of Hell are stronger than you. You are on my side, so I do not need to be afraid. In fact, I have confidence in your protection. It will never fail or run out.

In the darkness, you can see. When monsters lurk around, you already have them cornered. My mind is put at ease because you have looked under my bed and cleared out all of the things that go bump in the night. You truly are our Father. As my earthly father would tuck me in at night, turn on my night light, and tell me that I was safe, you constantly comfort me. You tell me not to fear because you have already handled my problems. You tell me to take heart because you have overcome the world.

When Jesus defeated sin and death, He also defeated fear. There is nothing on Earth, nor any principalities of Hell that can make me afraid. Through the power of your Holy Spirit, I rebuke all fear. I rebuke every attack of the enemy that tries to make me find safety by other means. The enemy wants me to feel safe in my own abilities or cleverness. He wants me to find security in relationships or in manmade objects. He uses the world to remind me that if I have so much money in my bank account or so many friends in my contact list, I will be safe.

Yet, I know that safety and security only come from you. Only you can keep me from being afraid. Help me to ignore the voices in my head that tell me to find safety elsewhere. You are the only one who can protect me from harm.

Amen.

WEEK 2

Dear God,

You have increased my faith over the last few months, and you have constantly reminded me of your faithfulness. You have supported me in every single situation and directed my path at every juncture. No matter where I go, you are there. Because of your faithfulness, I know that nothing can scare me. You are my protection.

Sometimes I wonder if it is cheating to say I have faith in you because of what I have seen. Then again, I have never physically seen you. I have only seen situations work out when I know they have been prayed for. I have only seen the results of your work, but not the hands that have done the work. I have felt your peace in times when it does not make any sense to experience it. When I look back over every situation, I can attribute the positive results to your grace and the negative results to my stupidity.

All this to say, I trust in your faithfulness, Lord. There are biblical accounts of you rescuing people from armies and restoring hope to broken people. Through you, a young boy defeated a giant warrior. Through you, a young Jewish woman stopped a genocide plot against her people. Through you, a prostitute was included into the genealogy of your son because she protected Israelite spies.

You are faithful to your people and you protect them. That does not mean that they have no concerns or fears, but they do have the assurance that you have already taken care of their future. I know, Lord, that I do not need to fear because you are faithful to protect me. You are faithful to work out the details of my future. You are faithful to end my sadness and restore my joy. There is so much that I do not understand and so much that can discourage my heart, but you are always there to uplift me.

I also know, Lord, that you do not abandon me because of my fear. Some people would say that being afraid means our relationship with you is failing and being with you means we will never be afraid again. When we do fear, we feel that we are unworthy of your presence and your grace. The more I get to know you, though, the more I realize that you do not give up on us if we succumb to human emotions. You do not want us to be robots who do not ever experience fear or worry. You do not punish us for being afraid.

Instead, as a father comforts his child, you ease our minds. We do not *need* to fear, but even if we do you are there to soothe us. Fear does not have to overwhelm us or cause us grief, but we also do not have to worry that even having far in our hearts means we are failing you.

We do not need to fear retribution. We do not need to fear that you are going to leave us on our own in the wilderness. You will constantly be surrounding us and protecting us from our enemies. You will lead us into battles that we know will be won because you are our General. You will use us to comfort others and show them how your perfect peace has driven out our fear.

Even when I am afraid, I will find joy in your faithfulness. I have your promises and assurances that no weapon formed against me shall prosper. Most importantly, I am confident that neither height nor depth, nor anything in all of creation will be able to separate me from your love.

Amen.

WEEK 3

Dear God,

This week, I am reminded that the fear of you is the beginning of wisdom. I know, Lord, that the word "fear" does not mean that I need to be afraid of you. Rather, it is a sign of respect and reverence. In fact, when I am in tune with your Spirit, I fear nothing, but I respect you. I reverently worship and adore you; I am in awe of you. When I read your Word and understand everything you have done for your people since the beginning of time, I am amazed. How marvelous and wonderful is your love for your people! How wise are your ways!

Even when you created Adam and Eve, you knew that they may fail you. You could have taken away their freewill and made them follow your commands to the letter, but you did not do that. You did not want them to be puppets or dolls. You desired that they love you and obey you with their whole hearts because they chose to, not because you made them. They messed up, they brought sin into the world, and that could have been the end of the story. You could have left us to our own devices and given up on humanity, but instead you continued to uplift your people. You saved Noah's family and two of every living creature. You led Abraham and Sarah to a new land, where you increased their family to number more than the stars in the sky. Your servant Joseph was able to establish his entire family in Egypt after you faithfully delivered him from his enemies.

When Egypt enslaved your people, you heard their cries and led them out of slavery. Through your servant Moses, you delivered them from Pharaoh's wickedness, and saved them from death. Even when they complained and grumbled against you, you provided their every need with manna and quail. You established a Sabbath to break their mentality of slavery. You set them free.

I can read all of that just in the first two books of your Word, and if that were all I knew about you, I would still be amazed. Every single situation you worked out for the good of your people and the glory of your name. You are the ultimate Author and Master. Nothing was too difficult for you then, nor is it too difficult for you now.

You did not stop there, though. When we were lost to sin and shame, you sacrificed your only son to bring us closer to you. You shattered the gates of Hell, and you destroyed the power of death. Father, because of your sacrifice, I get to worship you today. I get to call you mine, as you call me yours. How could I not be in awe of that? How could I not "fear" you for your greatness?

The truth is, I often take you for granted. Sometimes I even attribute your works to other entities. Even if I am just being sarcastic, I often say things like, "the universe is looking out for you today," or "you must have offended the sun god." I do not believe in the "universe" or any other gods, but sometimes I just let these silly sayings slip out of my mouth. On the other hand, sometimes I blame you for things that you did not cause. You are good. You cannot be evil, and you cannot create evil. Forgive me for the times that I have blamed you for things that were the result of sin in the world. Help me to put more respect on your name.

You are awesome, and you are the only one worthy of that title. I am filled with wonder when I reflect on who you are. I respect you and will follow your commands because I know that you are good. Sin has no hold on me because you have destroyed its power in my life. I fear you, Lord. I praise you for your awesome power. Help me to continue in your ways, Lord. Keep my feet from stumbling. All I want to do is honor you.

Amen.

WEEK 4

Dear God,

I love knowing that the future is already in your hands. It is such a comfort to me that I do not have to fear tomorrow because you are already there. Still, there are times when I do fear the future because so much has happened in the past. What we went through with a global pandemic was terrifying. That is a piece of history I hope that we never repeat again. There is also racial disparity still happening, and I fear the consequences of not loving our brothers and sisters.

I fear the attacks that the enemy keeps trying to rain down. One day, the world as we know it will come to an end and the Devil will reign on the throne. Even though I know that in that time you will defeat him and bring your children to Heaven to dwell with you, I fear that day. I am scared that I will see that happen in my lifetime and I will not be able to protect my loved ones.

On that note, I am afraid of losing my loved ones. My earthly relationships are so valuable, and it is my support system that has helped me through my darkest moments. My family members are my rock. Even when we annoy each other and infuriate each other, they are the earthly resources I turn to most for wisdom and comfort. Losing any of them would throw my life off balance and I would feel lost.

My closest friends are the family members I got to choose. They are like-minded and kind. They keep me accountable and tell me when I am being foolish. We have had so many highs and lows together, and I cannot imagine what my life would be like if they had not been there for me. If I knew that a future was coming without my closest friends present, I would not want that future. I would rage against that future because I would not have my tribe with me.

Often, I am afraid of suffering. I have seen people get tortured or even murdered for their faith. I have witnessed distant relatives and acquaintances deal with long-term illnesses. Cancers and organ failures and mysterious diseases frighten me. I often consider what would happen if I had a silent illness that no doctor could identify and I died because they could not figure out what was wrong with me. Truthfully, I am afraid of death. I am also afraid of death being slow and painful. When I do die one day, I want it to be quick and painless.

Of all these things I fear, Lord, I know that they are not worth my mental energy. You determine my future and there is little I can do to create the future I want. I cannot stop death, I cannot protect my loved ones, and I cannot ensure that the world does not end up in total chaos and devastation. I cannot know your plans, and it is not my job to.

Forgive me for carrying around so much fear and not surrendering it to you. Forgive me for the times I have not trusted you to take care of my every need. I repent of my fears, and I want to spend the rest of my life trusting you, no matter how crazy things get around me. I accept your comfort and your peace, and the fact that you control the future. I will not be afraid because you do not want that for me. You simply want me to trust in you and let you worry about the rest. Help me to do that, Lord, so that our relationship may become even better.

Amen.

7

JULY - JOY

WEEK 1

*D*ear God,

Like Job, there are times when I feel that every good thing has been taken from me. During the COVID-19 pandemic of 2020-2021, it seemed that every time I put hope in something, it was dashed. I was unhappy to the point of depression. I was grieved and heartbroken. There have been many times in my life where I have felt that same weight. Depression can sit on my chest until I cannot breathe. It can squeeze out every single positive thought in my head. It can make the world seem darker and less friendly.

Then you come in and restore my joy. You may not give me back everything that was taken away as you did with Job. In fact, I may gain nothing material at all. That is not where my joy comes from. My joy comes from you alone. Only you can restore joy in my heart and give me a reason to dance.

Even when everyone in the world is lost in their despair, you give your people joy. Your Spirit lightens their hearts. Your promises remind us that there is so much to hope for. Your joy is our strength. You give it abundantly and often without us having to ask. You love blessing us with your joy.

I think of babies and how their joy is so palpable. Everything to them is so new and exciting. Every new skill they learn and moment they experience is another opportunity to find delight and joy. When they see their parents walk into the room, there is instant joy. When they meet people who show them love and admiration, they are filled with joy. When someone teaches them a new game or shows them something silly, they laugh with a joy that is absolutely contagious.

When I experience your joy, Lord, I am like a baby. I am not self-conscious or afraid of what anyone might think. My heart is so light and so excited in your presence. Like David, I will dance around like a fool. I will not worry what anyone thinks or has to say about me because I am rejoicing in you.

The world is full of sadness and pain. It constantly barrages us with awful images and messages and wants us to feel the full weight of its negativity. You, Lord, give us an incomparable joy. We are not concerned with the things of this world because we are too busy finding joy in your presence. We are not weighed down by burdens, instead we are uplifted by your promises. Your faithfulness is great, and your joy is certain. I will not fear because you have filled me with joy.

Amen.

WEEK 2

Dear God,

My joy is derived from you. The joy of you is my strength and salvation. I delight myself in your Word and feel the happiness that comes from knowing and loving you. We so often neglect to talk about your joy. We talk about your love and your peace, your compassion and your faithfulness, but we never sit around talking about the joy we find from your presence.

It is silly how joyful we can become. It does not make sense to anyone who does not know you. Even when we are afflicted with depression and anxiety that literally messes up the chemicals in our brains that help us feel happiness, we experience your joy. We understand that happiness is fleeting, but your joy is forever.

I can feel happy when someone gives me a gift, but that happiness will fade as the gift gets used. I can feel happy that I got a promotion at work, but that happiness will turn to stress as I accept my new responsibilities. Happiness is conditional, but your joy is not. It does not require any extraordinary circumstances or performative gestures. I do not need anything else to feel your joy. You bestow it in a way that shows us it is enough.

Your joy strengthens me in difficult times. As I said last week, Lord, the world is a negative place. I simply have to turn on the news to see devastation and trauma. Hearing of the loss that so many people face on a daily basis, I could feel great sadness. I could feel like life has no purpose and it is not worth sticking around for. Yet your joy surrounds me and shows me that life is precious. You created us and put us on this Earth for a purpose, and while we are here, we simply need to find strength in your joy.

Despite the great evil in this world, you rejoice over your people. You delight in them and celebrate with them. We experience your joy simply because we are alive and in this world you created. We can see the good in every situation because your joy has allowed us to do so. At the end of a long day, we can see your beautiful painting of a sunset and feel your joy. At the end of a treacherous night, we witness your sunrise and feel joy that you have blessed us with another day of life. When new life enters the world, we rejoice in the future that you have created for us.

Because of your joy, I know that I can survive whatever the world throws at me. Even in times of great worry and despair, your joy will fill me and comfort me. You will put a new song in my heart and keep me worshipping in spirit and in truth. How blessed I am to be in your presence and delight in your promises. Your joy is my strength and my song, and I will always be grateful that you have given it to me.

Amen.

WEEK 3

Dear God,

You formed Adam out of the dust and put your breath into his lungs. You gave him dominion over all other living creatures and put him in charge of your creation. Even when he failed you miserably, you continued to love him and protect him. You do the same for us, and we fail you on a daily basis.

It is hard to comprehend, Lord, that we could bring you joy. Sure, it makes sense for you to rejoice when one of your children has returned to the fold. Like the father of the prodigal son, you stand out in the field and watch for their return. When they come back, you throw them a party and rejoice over them. That I understand. It is something to celebrate to see your children come home. Why should you rejoice over me, though? I am nothing and no one. I am sinful, deceitful, and often hurtful. I break your heart all the time.

Still, you sing songs over me. You delight in our time together. You bless me and restore my hope. Why should you do this for me? Why should you love me and have joy because of me? Though I will likely never know or understand, I do want to be someone who actively brings you joy. That begins by asking you to forgive me of all my sins and actively pursue a relationship with you.

Your presence is so often something I take for granted. You could take away your Spirit from us at any time, and then what would we have? Nothing but sorrow and weeping for the rest of our lives. In order to bring you joy, I must take advantage of every second I have to spend with you. I must prioritize our relationship and strive to not sin against you.

I must also actively praise you. Lord, so often you perform miracles in my life and I do not praise you for them. Even the smallest acts that you perform for me are miraculous. I do not need to see seas being parted or dead men rising to experience your miracles in my life. If only I opened my eyes, I could see them every day. I need to make sure that when I do, I am pouring out praise and adoration to you.

Help me to bring you joy by my encounters with other people. Do not let me engage in toxic or sinful behaviors. Let my interactions be edifying and honoring to you. Let my conversations bring you joy because they are about you and your power in my life. May the words of my mouth and the meditations of my heart be pleasing to you. May they bring you joy because they are focused on you.

Lord, may I bring you joy in my decisions. It is not easy to stay on a right path, and often I make mistakes that lead me outside of your plan. Yet even then you have a backup plan for me, if only I choose to accept it. May I always decide to live within your will because that will bring you joy. May I always decide to spend more time with you, to have more conversations about you, and to give more of myself in helping your people.

I truly want to bring you joy in everything I do. I know that I cannot earn your grace or your love. I am not trying to be a better person because I think it will lead to better things in my life. I do not think that by bringing you joy I am meriting extra favor from you. It is completely the opposite. Because you have given so much to me already, I want my life to bring you joy. Though I can never earn what you have freely bestowed, I want my life to honor you. May I strive for a life that brings you nothing but joy.

Amen.

WEEK 4

Dear God,

Even though joy only comes from you, help me to bring that joy to others. I know that if I am a vessel of your Spirit, I can share your joy with so many. Joy is so much more permanent than happiness. It is not a fleeting feeling or a temporary state of being. Joy is a permanent state that comes from knowing you. I realize, then, that those who do not know you do not experience true joy. Their feelings of happiness come from temporary things, so their disappointment will be imminent. They will be looking to replicate the feeling of joy and find that it is nowhere to be found.

Let me be a messenger of your joy. Let me joyfully intercede on behalf of your children who need extra prayer and guidance. So many people need to know and experience the joy that you bring. The world is such a dark and lonely place without it. With it, though, it is like we are living in a world that others cannot see. We are experiencing a world of joy that only exists for those of us in the know. God, I want to bring more people into the know. I want the world to be full of people who can feel your joy.

That means that I will often have to do things that are difficult or make me feel uncomfortable. I will have to have conversations about you that some people are not going to want to hear. I will have to build relationships with people that I would otherwise never associate with. I will have to go out to the darkest places in the world to shed your light.

Help me to do so with a joyful spirit. It could be easy to feel like doing these tasks is a burden or an unwanted responsibility. I could grumble and complain when you command me to go and preach the gospel to those who have ears to hear it. Instead, Lord, help me to joyfully accept whatever mission you have for me. Give me a cheerful heart that lets me minister to others. May I never grow tired of doing your good deeds.

May my joy be so contagious, people have no choice but to catch it. May my love for you be so palpable that people feel it as soon as they meet me. Help me cheerfully give to them. Do not let me withhold any of your gifts out of selfishness or greediness. You have not given me yourself so that I can hoard you and hide you away. There is so much of you to go around. You have so much love and joy that the Earth will never be able to contain it all. So let me give it out as if it were free candy. Let me spread it around to everyone I meet.

What I love the most about your joy, Lord, is that the more I spread it, the more I will experience. You will make my joy complete. Just when I think I have experienced the depth of your joy, you will increase it beyond what I could have ever imagined. You want us to experience your joy and delight in it. You want us to be encouraged and uplifted daily.

I know, Lord, that I lack nothing from you. every good and perfect thing comes from you, including your matchless joy. I would be negligent if I did not share that with others. Let me cheerfully go into the world, knowing your joy is always with me.

Amen.

8

AUGUST - ENCOURAGEMENT

WEEK 1

*D*ear God,

You know how weak I am. You know my threshold for resisting temptations is so low at times. I know the right things to do, but often the wrong things seem so appealing at the time. Like the Apostle Paul, I know the good but often choose the bad.

You know I get so weary in doing good. I feel like giving up, falling on the side of the road, and not continuing in the work you have called me to do.

It is so hard sometimes; I see people succeeding when they are corrupt, those who profit from the misery of others. People who do not listen to my carefully given advice and make great mistakes that they could have avoided. I get tired, so tired.

Is this the way Elijah felt? He had done great, mighty things for you. He had proven your power to the pagan worshipers of Baal, and he had won great victories. And yet, as soon as he heard that Jezebel was threatening to come after him in retaliation, he retreated to a cave and had his own version of a pity party before You O Lord. "I have had enough!" he said to you. "I have been very zealous for the Lord God Almighty. The Israelites have rejected your covenant, torn down your altars, and put your prophets to death with the sword. I am the only one left, and now they are trying to kill me, too."

How often have I felt this way, like I was the only one trying to win victories, and now was all alone. How often have I said to you, "I have had enough." But you, God, spoke to Elijah, cared for him, allowed him his time of fear and pity, then showed him that he was not alone. You showed up and encouraged him in his time of weakness. When I have "had enough," you show me that there is so much more! You show me that others are on the same journey and you even send those to encourage me as you did when you sent Elisha to encourage Elijah. We are truly never "on our own."

In Isaiah 40:31 you tell me, "But they that wait upon the Lord shall renew their strength. They shall mount up with wings like eagles, They shall run and not be weary, They shall walk and not faint." Help me to hold on to that promise. Help me to accept your encouragement and thrive in its manifestation. You are my encouragement when I feel bereft of courage. Help me to accept those times of retreat to cry out to you and to have my strength renewed.

In times of weariness, let me rely on your strength. When I have reached my limit, remind me that you have more to give me. You give me more grace, more strength, more endurance, more comfort, and more encouragement. You help me through the worst of times, even when I neglect to turn to you. You encourage my spirit when I am downtrodden so that I can turn around and encourage others.

I long for that, Lord. It is my desire to be an encouragement so that you can better utilize me for your kingdom.

Amen.

WEEK 2

Dear God,

Sadness is a reality of life, I suppose. I am sad over lost opportunities, lost relationships, and lost loved ones. Sometimes grief fills me to a point that is unbearable. Though I know sadness comes mightily, I am often taken aback by it. It takes my breath away and I begin to doubt every promise you have ever made to me.

When the two followers walked that road to Emmaus after the crucifixion, you showed up and walked beside them. What kind of conversation is this that you have with one another as you walk and are sad? You walked beside them! You allowed them to express their sadness over the death of Jesus, and you let them talk it all out. Oftentimes when we are sad, we do not feel we can express it to anyone around us. We internalize it, we sorrow in it, we are brought low in our sadness. You allowed them to share their grief with you.

The old hymn says, "What a Friend we have in Jesus, all our sins and griefs to bear, what a privilege to carry, everything to God in prayer" (Wheeler et al., 1915). Thank you, Lord, that you walk beside me in my sadness and grief. Thank you that I am privileged to be able to carry all of this directly to you.

When the disciples' eyes were opened as to who you were, they realized that you had relieved their sadness. What joy they felt seeing you return. What encouragement they received in your presence.

Lord, help me to share with you all of my grief and all of my sadness, even if no one else seems to be there for me. This is my privilege as a child of God to come directly to you: to talk it out, to express it. Then Lord, also remind me to be still and listen to you. Let me allow you to encourage me in my sadness and to burn within me.

You went on to ask your disciples why they were troubled and downhearted. You told them to behold your scarred hands and feet and take encouragement from your defeat of death. They witnessed that everything you had told them was true. Every promise you made about yourself had come to pass. Though they witnessed your crucifixion and death, they also got to bear witness to your resurrection and victory.

Help me to recognize you as the risen Lord and be encouraged by your presence. I take reassurance that if I am of good courage and wait on you, you will bring hope to my spirit. I am also encouraged that you have shown your face to me. Why is my soul downcast, why am I so disturbed? As a deer pants for water, so my soul longs for you, and you do not withhold your presence from me.

When I am sad, I simply must look into the very face of God. My hope is in you. That is my encouragement and our peace. When I am sad, I can reach out to you. I can be still in your presence and know that you are in charge of everything. I know I can turn my eyes upon you and the things of this world will grow dimmer. Your face is so glorious and so bright that nothing can hold a candle to it. Help me, Lord, to keep my eyes on your glorious face, even when I am sad.

Amen.

WEEK 3

Dear God,

Discouragement is a large issue for me. It is so much a part of my daily walk. It is easy for me to become discouraged when I see the brokenness in the world or when I do not get what I want. People can also be a huge discouragement to me.

Sometimes, I am discouraged by their words. They tell me flat out that I cannot do what I set my mind to, or I am worthless. They tell me that I will not measure up to them or others. They tell me that I do not have the talent or ability to achieve my dreams. Other times, they discourage me with their lack of support. I will be so excited to present my friends and family a new idea. Rather than being excited for me, they tell me not to get ahead of myself. By not supporting me, they are discouraging me for chasing after something I long for. That something could be your will, Lord, but I listen to their words tell me I am a fool for trying.

There are certainly times I am discouraged. Times when I have lost confidence or enthusiasm. Lord, help me to come to you in those times. Help me to do the work to fight discouragement. Help me to see the value of self-care, first of all. I find that I get most discouraged when I am overtired, overcommitted, or undernourished. My spirit depends upon my body for these things. So help me to get proper rest, proper nutrition, and proper exercise. These things release things within my body that build up my spirit and help me to overcome discouragement.

Help me to always take the time to reflect on the Word that teaches me how to combat discouragement. When Jesus was preparing the disciples for His own departure, He said some pretty amazing things that continue to reach off the pages to me today.

Firstly, He said, "Peace I leave with you. My peace I give to you; not as the world gives do I give to you. Let not your heart be troubled, neither let it be afraid" (John 14:27, NIV). He also said to them, "And I will pray to the Father and He will give you another Helper that He may abide with you forever. I will not leave you orphans, I will come to you" (John 14:15-16, 18, NIV).

Despite my sadness, my grief, my overwhelming anguish, and discouragement, you have bestowed to me your peace. You are my ever-present help in hard times. You never intended that we should walk this path alone. Over and over in your Word, you admonish us with the great care you give even to the birds of the air and the grass of the field. The message is, with your great care for all of this, how much more you care for us, those created in your image.

So, I will walk closely with you and not get discouraged. I will take care of the temple that contains your Spirit. I will spend time in your Word listening to all that you have said to encourage me. You are my encourager and my spirit lifter. Help me to turn to you first in times of discouragement, rather than waiting for someone else to save the day. Let me not put my faith or hope into anyone else, because I know that they will fail me. I want to only find my encouragement from your presence.

Amen.

WEEK 4

Dear God,

I am surely not the only one who gets discouraged. I am part of the human family, and we are more alike than different. There are many others who also, like Elijah, feel that they are the only ones left fighting for righteousness. Help me live a life that shows to them that they are not alone.

You created us to be in union with you, but also to be in union with one another. You tell us that we are the body of Christ and we need every part to work. When our brothers and sisters are feeling hopeless or discouraged, I can be there to give them encouragement. When they are suffering, I can help lighten their load. Help me Lord to see the suffering in my fellow man. Help me to be strong enough to help people during these times. It would be so easy to turn my back on them and not offer any help or hope. I could easily say that it is someone else's problem and walk away during their time of need. How opposite of Christ that would be. It is not who I want to become.

In the same ways that I get discouraged, others do, too. Sometimes I need a hand to lift me up in my spirit, and sometimes I need to be that hand to lift someone else up. There are many who seem to have hit a brick wall. They do not see that there is hope on the other side of that wall. They need someone to point out the door, the gate, and the ladder to get them to the other side.

I have been at that wall so many times. The wall of unfulfilled dreams, the wall of underachieved goals, or the wall of high expectations. Many times I confess that I have been guilty of putting the bricks into that wall and become imprisoned by walls of my own making. Yet I know there is always a way. So many times you have sent people into my life to help me burst through those walls. Help me to be that person for those who need it.

The amazing thing about humanity is that you have created us with such similar needs, dreams, hopes, and yes, problems. The human experience is a common experience that we share. Make me brave enough to help others get through their walls the way you have sent so many to help me through my own. Make me your hands and feet, your mouthpiece, and your heart. Tell me exactly what to say that would uplift someone else, or shut my mouth if they do not need words.

More often than not, encouragement comes from what we do not say. It comes from getting down in the trenches with someone and supporting them. People do not need to hear that their situation will get better, or that everything will be okay. I know that in the depths of my discouragement, that has been the last thing I have wanted to hear. When the time comes for me to be your representative of encouragement, help me to know whether that requires words or actions. Do not let me say or do anything that would make someone's situation even worse.

Lord, make me an instrument of your divine love. Help me to be a calming and soothing presence. As your words are often a balm for my soul, use your words through me to be a divine balm for someone else. Let me be a harbinger of good news, a drop of sunshine for someone who is dealing with a massive rain cloud. It is only by your Spirit that I can become these things, so keep me in tune with you. When you specifically send me to encourage someone in need, may I be obedient and willing to do so. May I never refuse anyone a touch of your joy.

You tell me that as a Christian, it is my spiritual duty to uplift my brothers and sisters. Regularly I am reminded that I need to be a support to someone who needs help carrying a heavy load. So many of my brothers and sisters are carrying burdens that I will never see or understand, and it is only in your wisdom that I will know how to be there for them. Help me to be a burden bearer, Lord. Help me to be an encourager. Help me to give as has been given to me. Help me to help others get to the other side of their brick walls.

Amen.

9

SEPTEMBER - LOVE

WEEK 1

*D*ear God,

Throughout the last seven months, you have continued to remind me of your immeasurable love. Your love is overwhelming and everlasting. It is unconditional and perfect. I meditate often on how little you expect from me in return. You want me to love you back, but even if I did not, your feelings would not change. You would still cover me in your love and continue to pursue me.

You loved me so much that you sent your Son to die for my sins. I was a sinner, lost to the world, and condemned to the pits of Hell. We would have been separated for all of eternity, but you did not want that. Because of your love, you made the ultimate sacrifice and showed us what real love is. That agape love drives out fear, forgives sins, and accepts me as I am. It tells me that I am cherished, and there is nothing I could do to make you stop loving me.

That does not mean I do not infuriate you sometimes. As any child could irritate a parent with their disobedience, I often get on your nerves. So often I fail to love you as I should or to love your people as I should. Sometimes I get lost in my sin and turn my back on you. In those moments, your love for me does not waver. You do not suddenly decide that you have had enough of me and abandon me to my own devices. When I have come to my senses and repented of my sins, you are right there with open arms, waiting to tell me how much you love me.

Who else will ever love me like you do? No one ever could. I could have the most perfect, wonderful spouse in the world, and our love for each other would not even be a fraction of your love for us. If you could measure the amount of love in the entire world, it still would not equal your love. How incomparable and unimaginable is your amount of love.

We have all sinned and fallen short of your glory, and you still lavish us in your love. You still fight for us and protect us from evil. Your love remains steadfast through our sin and our failures, and you never give up on us. When we run away from you, your love chases after us and overtakes us. When we forsake you and curse your name, your love forgives us and extends to us grace.

We do not deserve to be loved by you. I do not deserve it, and I never could. Your love is not afraid of my failure, though. You are always reminding me that your love covers my sin. Your perfect love drives out all fear. Your love never fails me, even when I fail you. All of this love is unconditional and holy because you are love. It is not just part of your nature; it is your nature. Because of your love, you created the world and all of us in it because you wanted to share your love with us. You had a perfect union as the Holy Trinity, but you brought creation into that love and set us apart from all the other beings on Earth.

How could you love us? We may never know. It makes no sense. We give you nothing in return, and often flat out disrespect you. We give you our anger and our hatred, and still you choose to love us. We are often ashamed of how we treat you, but you forgive us and take away our shame. Even though we cannot even give you back a fraction of the love you give us, you do not mind. There are not enough words in all the languages of the world to express how grateful we are and humbled we are to be loved by you.

Amen.

WEEK 2

Dear God,

I know that I will never be able to love you as much as you love me. My love will never be as faithful and pure. Often, I demonstrate a lack of love with my actions. I turn away from you or treat you with indifference. I empty my schedule of you and instead fill it up with other things that are not worthy of my time. This is not how I show you love, and it certainly is not how you have called me to love you.

You want me to love you with my whole heart, mind, and soul. Firstly, I consider my heart which is so full of different kinds of love. The love I have for my family is slightly different than what I have for my friends. With my family, I know that I could never stop loving them, even if sometimes I do not always like them. We are bound by blood and we will always exist in each other's lives, whether we want to or not. Mostly, though, I love them with a never-ending love that spans time and distance. No matter where I am in the world, I will love my family members and cherish their presence in my life.

Though I usually love my friends in a similar manner, sometimes my love for them is a little more conditional. Often, I make friends because of the similarities I have with them, but those similarities do not always last. Sometimes we grow and change; a day comes when I realize that my friend and I are too different, and my love for them has decreased. I never intentionally want to stop loving my friends, but sometimes it happens without any conscious thought.

Then, of course, there is romantic love. This is a hard love to deal with sometimes because there are so many emotions attached to it. Sometimes my "love" is based on physical attraction and desire. I know this is not truly love, but it is a consuming lust. Unfortunately, that lust can turn into obsession, and my brain and heart are confused as to whether I am in love or just obsessed. This love can also be conditional and even dangerous. In some romantic relationships, I have let my love for this person allow me to accept poor treatment. Other times, I have treated them poorly and still called it "love." I have not always demonstrated the kind of love you want me to show to a romantic partner, and for that I am sorry.

Loving you with my whole heart can be difficult because, as you see, it is so full of other people and different types of love. Loving you with my whole mind is even harder. My mind is often filled with distractions and sometimes filth. Often, Lord, I fill my mind up with images and thoughts that I know are not honoring to you. Sometimes those thoughts and images are based on the lust I am harboring in my heart; other times they come from anger or selfishness.

In Romans 12:2 (NIV), Paul reminds your followers to, "be not conformed to the pattern of this world, but be transformed by the renewing of your mind." God, I know that if I am to love you with my whole mind, I must renew my mind. Every day, I will need to wipe it clean and start fresh with thoughts that are holy and honoring. I need to meditate on your Word so that my mind can be turned to you.

Finally, loving you with my whole spirit can be difficult because there are so many distractions in the world. Our culture promotes so many other religions and idolatry that are not pleasing to you, and sometimes I get caught up in the popularity. Sometimes, my spirit becomes diluted with TV shows I watch or music I listen to that makes me doubt your sovereignty. Lord, forgive me when I let my spirit be led astray by other entities, and help me to stand firm in your love.

Father, I truly want to love you with my whole heart, mind, and spirit. I want to please you, honor you, trust you, and declare your love to others. Though I am prone to wander, I ask you to seal my heart. Help me to prioritize my relationship with you and my love for you above all else.

Amen.

WEEK 3

Dear God,

In First John, we learn that if we hate our brother, we cannot know you because you are love. How often do I treat my brothers and sisters with hate or indifference? More often than I would like, for sure. People are so difficult to love sometimes, but I know you know that full well. Your ability to love us despite our stupidity is truly hard to fathom. We spend so much time failing you and breaking your heart, but you still choose to love us, and it is incredible.

I want to love others that way, too. Help me to develop that agape love that provides unconditional, unselfish love. I do not want to love people in a selfish way. That is how the world loves, and it is not the example you want for us to follow. The world tells us that we are worth loving if we are beautiful, rich, or powerful. Everyone else is not worth the time or effort. It is easy for so many of us to feel unloved by the world because that is the lesson we are taught.

I think about those people the world really hates. The prostitutes, drug addicts, homeless, and downtrodden. These are people we avert our eyes from and walk quickly past. We want nothing to do with them, and we usually have no kind word to give or change to spare for them. In conversations with like-minded individuals, we talk about how it is their fault they are in these situations, or we speculate that they will use our money to fuel their addictions.

I think about single mothers who are working several jobs just to make ends meet. They have to rely on food stamps and other government-funded programs so they can feed and house their children. They are just trying their best, but we sit around judging them and calling them "lazy." Sometimes, their children are hyperactive or downright wild, and we click our tongues and call for better discipline.

God, you have called us to love these people. Every single one of them. You have called us to love murderers and government officials and policemen and members of the LGBTQ community. You have called us to love people who do not look like us, worship like us, or think like us. Father, I have been so bad about loving your children. I have neglected to show them love because I was too caught up in judging them and treating them harshly. Some of them I do not spare a passing thought to. My indifference toward so many groups of people speaks to my intense lack of agape love.

Forgive me for every single person I have failed to love. Forgive me for my lack of compassion and my overabundance of judgement toward them. Forgive me for the hateful and ignorant words I have spoken about them. Help me to love them like you love them. Help me to see them, not as the world sees them, Lord, but how you see them. They are your creation. You died for them just as you died for me. You forgave their sins and poured out your love for them just as you did for me. I am unworthy of your love, yet I treat them like they are unworthy of mine.

Anything that I do that lacks your love is worth nothing. Any help I provide or kindness I show that lacks your love is worthless. Help me to show your love to others in a way that is radical and revolutionary, just as your love is for us. From me to be an instrument of your love.

Amen.

WEEK 4

Dear God,

Increase my ability to love. As you know, I am often selfish and prideful. I have a hard time loving others as I am much more prone to judge and argue. I see the perfect love you have for me and my fellow man, and I often reject it. When it comes to showing your love to others, I can be cruel or cowardly. Cruel to withhold the news of that love or cowardly by being too afraid to approach people.

Yet, I want to be able to love more. I want to love you more and love my neighbors more. I want to put that love into action and find ways to serve you better. You said that whatever I do for the least of humanity, I am doing for you. Help me to love those who the world has deemed unlovable. Out of that love, help me to be compassionate to them. Do not let me be afraid or anxious when approaching someone in love. Give me boldness and authority because I am standing on your Word.

Give me the strength to love those who have wronged me. It is easy to wish these people harm or pray for their downfall, but that would not be a very loving response. In realizing that all human beings are flawed and make mistakes, maybe I can learn to be more loving toward my enemies. Increase my love for them, especially when they have only shown me hate or disdain. Help me to show them that their lack of love toward me cannot deter your Holy Spirit within me.

Give me the grace to love those that I just do not agree with. Over the last few years, people have gotten even more divisive about the smallest issues, and it is easy to spew hate toward one another. It is easy to categorize people into boxes based on what they believe and then write them off for those beliefs. I have done that often in the last few years, and because of it I have demonstrated a lack of love even to my Christian brothers and sisters. They are not my enemies, yet I treat them with the same amount of indifference or dislike that I would to an enemy. Help me to love them, even when I think they are wrong.

Help me to love myself more because I am a bearer of your image. The world wants me to believe I am not good enough or worthy to be loved, but you have already shown me that is not true. By dying on the cross for my sins, you proved that I am worth loving. As I grow to love myself more, help me to take care of my physical temple. Help me to honor and steward this body that you have given me, and appreciate it for everything it does for me.

God, I want to be so full of love that it does not make sense. I want people to question how I could love so much, and when they do, I want to point them to you. Increase your love in me so that I may show others the way to you.

Amen.

10

OCTOBER - PATIENCE

WEEK 1

*D*ear God,

Throughout my life, I have turned to you for so many things. I have presented so many dreams and desires to you and you have always answered them in the way that was most beneficial to me and glorifying to you. You have proven time and time again your faithfulness to me, even in the midst of my doubt. Still, I have hopes and dreams and desires that I worry over. I reluctantly surrender them to you with an anxious spirit. Until you answer those requests, and especially until you answer them in a way I hope, I generally fret over them. Rather than turning to you for answers and patience, I turn to everyone else and usually receive terrible advice.

A lot of times, though, I am told to wait patiently on you. Lord, you know that I am not a patient person. I want immediate solutions. What I worry about today, I want fixed today. That is not how you work, though. Your timing is different from mine and you are not concerned about deadlines. As the Creator, you are not constrained by my arbitrary timeline. If I am being honest, I often get frustrated having to wait on your answer.

All that is to say, Father, that I acknowledge that I need to increase my patience. I especially need to learn how to wait patiently on you. How arrogant of me to assume that my timing is better than yours. How foolish I am to give you a deadline. With some requests, I tell myself that if you have not answered by X date, it must not be your will. You must spend so much time laughing at me. It is not remotely up to me to decide what your will is. Until I hear from you, I just need to sit down and shut up.

In your Word, you tell me to be still and know that you are God. I must also acknowledge that I am not you. It is not up to me when prayers get answered and when the clock has run out on a prayer request. My dreams are not dashed because I have not heard from you by a certain date. That is such a human way of thinking. Your thoughts are so much higher than that.

Help me to be patient as I wait upon you. I already know that you are faithful to your promises, and you have promised so many good things for my future. In this time of waiting, help me to grow closer to you. I know that waiting does not mean I have to sit around and do nothing. In the period of waiting, you are calling me to do work for your kingdom. You have tasks and missions for me to carry out. While I am learning to be more patient as I wait upon you, I am also learning to be more obedient. Increase these virtues 10-fold so that when the waiting is over, I am ready to face whatever challenges you have, or enjoy whatever blessing you pour out.

Amen.

WEEK 2

Dear God,

You know more than anyone how infuriating humanity can be. People get on my nerves all the time. They never do what I hope they will. They are fallible and unreliable. God, I greatly lack patience toward others, but I know you want me to have it. How often do I treat your people unkindly or refuse to listen to them out of a lack of patience. Sometimes, I tell myself that it is okay to lose my patience with others because it is not that big of a sin. Then I remember that all sin is the same to you, and I need to work on my patience with others.

Sometimes, I grow impatient when I give someone advice and they do not follow it. I see that they are continuing down the same bad path for them and then complaining that nothing in their life is improving. How it bothers me, Lord. Why do people even ask for my opinions if they are going to do the opposite of what I say? Other times, people test my patience by making me wait. They are inconsistent and sometimes lazy. They say they will show up, but they do not. They say they are five minutes away, but really, they have not left yet. Am I meant to be a saint? Am I supposed to pretend that it does not bother me to have to wait for others?

My brothers and sisters in Christ can also be so hateful and cruel toward others. I feel as if I am the only one who has actually read your Word and is following the correct path. I want to correct them all and yell at them for being so dense. My anger shows my lack of patience, and I certainly do not have all the time in the world to correct their wrong thoughts. Am I my brother's keeper? Should I really have to be there to gently correct him in love if he is doing wrong?

Oh, Lord, you see the sinful trail of my thoughts. You witness over and over my lack of patience toward my fellow man. It must make you laugh to see how impatient I can be when I am sure I cause you the same amount of grief. How inconsistent I can be with you. How often do I hear your advice and do the exact opposite. How wrong my own thoughts and actions can be, and I have a complete unwillingness to accept it.

Help me to be more patient with others because you are so patient with me. Your patience is literally supernatural. You do not ask or require us to be perfect. You do not embarrass us when we get things wrong. So often I get things wrong. I am so arrogant in my ways sometimes. Often, I can be the worst offender of testing your patience. You never give up on me, though, and you never let your anger toward me get the best of you. Though I can never be completely like you, help me develop a higher level of patience. Help me to better take care of my brothers and sisters, even when they are working my last nerve.

Amen.

❧

WEEK 3

Dear God,

I certainly have a tendency to get ahead of myself when I am excited about something. I am like a child at Christmas who cannot wait to open his presents. They will snoop around the house trying to find all the secret hiding places. When they finally find their treasures, they secretly open them, then carefully rewrap them so they do not get caught. Though I know I cannot get away with that kind of behavior—because you see everything I do—I often burst with anticipation while waiting for the future.

You have made me promises about what to expect, and sometimes I want them right *now*! I do not want to wait for the future to come until I experience you pouring out your blessings upon me. I want to get to those glorious moments as soon as possible. Getting to those moments can feel like a race. Time goes by so slowly while I am waiting to experience your promises, and the waiting can feel useless. What am I supposed to learn during the wait? What is the point of sitting around doing nothing when I could be getting to the good stuff? These foolish thoughts run through my head, and my impatience grows even deeper.

I already know that you want me to be working during my time of waiting. I know that you have things for me to accomplish, you have parts of my character to develop. Still, I can get so bored or so anxious trying to keep my hands clasped in my lap. My time would be better spent chasing after the future, rather than being sat in a chair and being told to wait.

Sometimes, Lord, I lose myself in daydreaming about what my future could be. I ignore the present and important tasks that you have bestowed upon me. I neglect your people and let details slip through the cracks. I realize the amount of patience and grace you show toward me in those moments. I must be such a frustrating person, constantly trying to get to a certain point in time, rather than appreciating the blessings you have given me right now.

Father, forgive me in these times when my impatience gets the best of me. Forgive me when I try to fit your perfect plan into my imperfect timing. Lord, I test you so much. I ask for signs and wonders that you do not have to provide me. I expect you to work out everything, to take care of every detail, but I do not thank you for it. In my rush to get to my promised future, I step all over you and take advantage of your kindness to me.

I know that my future is in your hands and it will be amazing. Until then, though, help me to focus on the present moment. May I worship you more and appreciate you. May I show you love and refrain from asking you to align your will to my plans and my timeline. Let me not get so focused on the future that I forget to live in the present.

Amen.

WEEK 4

Dear God,

If there is one thing I have learned about you over the last few months, it is that you use difficult situations to shape our character. Lord, you know that my character still needs so much shaping. I am a lump of clay on your wheel, and I know that you are turning me into a masterpiece. You are forming me into the person that I need to be, and the best part is that I will never be finished. You will always be grooming me and changing me. Even then, though, you will still view me as precious. I do not have to be perfect for you to love me exactly as I am. What a relief because I am rife with imperfections!

God, my greatest desire is to be the person you want me to be, and I know that means that you are going to have to increase my patience. In order to do that, you are going to have to stretch me past my limits. You will have to force me out of my comfort zone and lead me into places I never imagined. In those places, though, you will be with me. You would never send me somewhere that your Spirit would not accompany me.

I will be light in dark places. I will be kind to difficult people. I will show love to those who only show hate. In all of these circumstances, you will be growing my patience and increasing my strength. When people reject me, help me to pursue them in love anyway. When they do not listen to wise counsel, help me to give it anyway. When they take for granted my time and my effort, help me to keep showing up and keep serving anyway.

Part of becoming more patient is realizing that people might walk all over me. The world will tell me to stand up for myself, to not allow that behavior. Sometimes, though, you will be asking me to stay and wait for your instruction. You may place me in a difficult position, serving difficult people for months or years at a time. I may be desperate to find a new situation, and you may constantly tell me "no." I will want to quit and run away, and those are exactly the moments when you will be developing my patience.

I know that making me more patient is not going to be an easy task for either of us. In your case, though, you will not mind the work. You will be thrilled to add things to my plate that will cause me to rely on you more. For me, though, I realize it is going to be unbearable at times. I will get frustrated and angry. I will grow weary of doing good.

In those moments, remind me how much I need you. Remind me how patient you are with me at all times, and that I wanted to become more patient. Remind me that the way of growth will contain hardships, but I will come out as a better person. In all things, increase my patience so that I may serve you better.

Amen.

WEEK 5

Dear God,

There have been so many moments in my life when I have experienced trials and afflictions. In those moments, I have wept and cursed bitterly. At times, I waited for the end to come, whether that meant the end of the trial or the end of my life. It was so easy to become downcast and downtrodden, and I was ready to give everything up out of my pain.

As I have gotten closer to you, I have been meditating on the words to "be patient in affliction." I am not patient under the best circumstances, but to be patient during times of distress is almost too much to ask. I want to be able to display that level of patience, that level of obedience, but I fall so much more than I stand.

As I get impatient waiting for the future, I get impatient waiting for my trials to end. In fact, sometimes the waiting feels unbearable. It is that same feeling of hearing nails on a chalkboard or being desperately hungry with nothing to eat. It is not always necessarily pain but often discomfort. Trying to endure that discomfort can feel unmanageable.

Even now as I pray, I am thinking about an affliction that is causing me stress. It is already known to you, and you already know how this situation is going to end. Though I feel like I am in the middle of the desert with no hope of rescue, you already see me prospering.

I know that you are trustworthy and faithful. This trial will not always last. Though weeping and sorrow come at night, your joy will come in the morning. Being patient until morning, though, is such a struggle. I am ready right now to feel the sun on my face. I am ready to have my heart uplifted and my joy restored.

Still, there is likely a reason you are asking me to wait. After all, I did just ask you to increase my patience. You are producing something good in me. You are allowing me to endure this affliction so that one day I may use my experience to help others. You are speaking to me and caring for me, showing me that you are always present and always comforting. Though I desperately want this trial to end, I also want to learn how to be content in your presence in all circumstances.

You have promised me that I will come out of this situation stronger. I will flourish, I will be renewed, and I will take delight in your ways. Until that moment comes, help me to be patient and wait on you. Give me the endurance to get to the end of this, and at that time, remind me that it only happened because of your strength and your faithfulness.

Amen.

11

NOVEMBER - WEAKNESS

WEEK 1

*D*ear God,

Over the last 10 months, you have made me so much stronger. I have grown closer to you, and I have learned to rely on your presence. My faith, love, and patience have all increased. God, you have proven to me that there is nothing you cannot do in my life and nothing I need to fear. That even includes my own weakness.

You know better than anyone how weak I have been in my life. I have been physically, spiritually, and mentally weak at different times. I have chosen to sin out of my spiritual weakness. I have chosen to be angry and mean-spirited out of my mental weakness. I have fallen and hurt myself because of my physical weakness.

Increase in me your strength for my whole being. It would not do if I were physically strong but spiritually weak. You want me to work on and develop strength in every facet of my life. You want my character to be strong. You want my faith to be strong. You want my love to be strong.

I know that I lack nothing in your presence. I know that if I ask, I shall receive. Now, I am asking you for more strength. I am asking you to make me the strong believer that you have always wanted me to be. At the same time, I acknowledge the great responsibility that comes with being strong. I have to be available to help other people lift their spiritual burdens. I have to be strong in the face of trials and temptations. I have to be an emotional support to those who are mentally weak. I have to be courageous for those who are weak in heart.

Even so, I still desire to be stronger. I desire to help my brothers and sisters in whatever way they need me. I desire for my spiritual life to be solid and firm. Each night, I want to be doing heavy lifting in reading your word. I want my time in prayer and the Scripture reading to strengthen my faith and resolve to be a better person. Let my relationship with you be the strongest and healthiest relationship in my life. Let me grow daily in your Word, realizing that there is not a limit to how deep our bond can grow if only we spend time together each day.

Help me to be supportive and emotionally available to the people who need me the most. It is tempting to keep all this strength to myself and not use it to help others, but you are challenging me to uplift my brothers and sisters. You want me to provide them care, even when they are at their worst. Sometimes that will require even a strong stomach. Hopeless people can end up in desperate situations that are difficult to witness. If no one else is willing or able to help in those times, let me go. Let me use your strength to help them.

Grow my strength in the face of temptation. I know that when I am successful in resisting temptation, it is only because you have given me the strength to do so. I cannot take pride in myself because my flesh is and always will be weak. It is only your Spirit within me that can give me strength.

Continue to strengthen me and grow me into the person I need to be. Let me always strive to be my best, not for my glory, but for yours.

Amen.

WEEK 2

Dear God,

When I try to imagine your strength, I find it to be unfathomable. You created the entire universe and you "have the whole world in your hands." Your character is unfailing; your promises are always sure. You are the strongest being in existence, there is no question about. The enemy tries to intimidate you. He tries to turn your people against you and raise up armies of evil to overpower you. Even if he could turn all living creatures against you, they would not be strong enough to defeat you. You can speak one word and all nations would crumble under the weight.

I am inspired and encouraged by your strength. It is unfailing and unwavering. Though my strength is often gone, yours never runs out. You have enough to give to everyone and still you do not run out. In fact, you promise to give your people strength. You encourage us that your strength can carry us through any problem we may face. It is incredible to think of how strong you are and understand that it is a major facet of your character. You cannot be weak. You cannot fail. God, you have toppled entire armies. You have cut off governments at their knees and restored hope to nations.

As strong as you are, though, you are also incredibly gentle. You understand and teach us that strength does not have to make you unapproachable. You do not shame us because you are strong and we are weak. Instead, in your strength, you comfort us. You have patience with us and forgive us, even when we are nothing but weak. Rather than crushing us under your feet, which you would have every right to do, you call us by name and lead us by still waters. You heal us and provide for us until we have enough strength to stand on our own.

What an amazing example you set for us. While so many use their strength and power to destroy and injure others, you use yours for the opposite. You empower and encourage your people. You protect them and keep them from falling. You surround them with love so that they always know they are not alone.

You also challenge us. In these last 11 months, I have consistently asked you to challenge me to make me better in different areas. In your strength, you have. You do not get jealous or fearful when I get stronger. Firstly, you know that I will never remotely match your strength. Yet you also *want* me to get stronger. You want me on your team, in your army. Even if I am physically the weakest person on the planet, you call me your own and empower me to fight. Any army in the world would reject me for my many physical failings, but you challenge me to be a soldier. The best thing is knowing that because I am on your side, I am already successful. The enemy has already fallen because of your power.

Father, I am absolutely humbled that you would want to call me your own. You have all the power and all the strength, and you certainly do not need me. Yet, you want me. You love me. It is unfathomable, but I am so grateful. As your child, may I work harder and grow stronger so that I may feel worthy of the responsibilities you have given me.

Amen.

WEEK 3

Dear God,

I love reading through the Psalms and seeing how David was constantly calling on you for strength. David, one of the true heroes of the Bible, knew where his strength came from. David, who as a young boy faced down a giant, and who as an adult had to run from King Saul who in jealousy wanted to kill him. David, who did succumb to temptation with Bathsheba and paid the price dearly, must have felt so weak and useless, like I do sometimes. He must have felt like a failure with no strength to go on. Yet, he was able to proclaim that he loved you and you were his strength. He called you his deliverer and his fortress. He trusted you because of your great strength.

He must have been physically exhausted from being on the run; his strength must have been depleted from hunger. He was probably mentally suffering from being isolated from his loved ones at home. Sorrow was likely sitting heavy on his chest. I, too, have been weak from physical exertion, lack of sleep, and periods of hunger. I have also felt isolated at times from my loved ones. I have felt the sting of betrayal that leaves me angry, hurt, and totally hollow.

In Psalm 29:11, David reminds us that you are the strength of your people. He knew from where to go to truly find strength. So often, Lord, I wander around in the web of my own bitter thoughts that leave me impotent and powerless. That is because there is no strength in that web. There is no strength in my bitterness or wounded feelings. There is truly only one source for strength.

David also reminds us that because you are our strength, we have nothing to be afraid. of. I do not need to be afraid of my own weakness, because in it you are providing me strength. You are giving me everything I need and I get to bask in the sweetness of your presence. When I am weak, I need to declare that boldly and exuberantly that my strength comes only from the Lord.

And you, God, are not only the physical strength but the strength of my heart. Psalm 73:26 says, "My flesh and my heart fail, but God is the strength of my heart and my portion forever" (NIV). So Lord, the lessons that I learn from David, the man after your own heart, are these:

You, O God, are my strength when I have sinned and do not have the strength to get back up.

You, O God, are my strength when I have been betrayed and can only think of revenge, bitterness, anger.

You, O God, are my strength when all of my own strength has been depleted, physically, emotionally, and spiritually. Your strength is perfect, most especially when my strength is gone. So, Lord, I will boast in my weakness, knowing that it will point people to your strength.

Amen.

WEEK 4

Dear God,

It is hard to wrap my head around the fact that Jesus was tempted just like me. Sometimes my temptations seem so overwhelming! Jesus, how did you turn down the temptation to turn the rocks into bread? I do not even have to be famished to be tempted to eat the wrong things, to even hide that from those around me. How did you resist the temptation to show off your power to have all creation worship you for the tricks you could do? And how did you not just bypass the cross altogether? Surely you could have proven your identity as the Messiah by calling down a battalion of angels and could have avoided the pain, the extreme suffering, the humiliation, and the momentary separation from God himself as you hung on that cross. Yet, you overcame the temptations to take the easy way out in every situation. You bore my sin on that cross in agony before the whole world.

I often choose the easy way out—a white lie to keep me from looking bad, engaging in idle gossip, looking the other way when I see people suffering. I have done things to make me look "cool" when you would have wanted me to stand apart and look different. I have often fallen into the trap of being "of the world," of desiring what the world desires and rejecting you for asking me to follow you.

Psalm 22:19 admonishes me by saying, "But You, O Lord, do not be far from Me; O my Strength, hasten to help me" (NIV). You are never further than a breath away from me, so why is it so hard to call on you to be my strength? Too often, I turn to other entities to be my strength. I put my faith in what I can see, rather than in you who I cannot. Though I know that you are right next to me at all times, my flesh wants to turn away from your Spirit. It wants to engage in the things that the world loves.

I want to rejoice with the psalmist who said, "The Lord is my strength and my shield; My heart trusts in Him and I am Helped; Therefore my heart greatly rejoices, and with my song I will praise Him" (Psalm 28:7, NIV). That is what I want, Lord. I want and need that strength to overcome—that strength to walk in your way. That strength that can cause me to rejoice.

Help me to remember the truth of I Corinthians 10:13, "No temptation has overtaken you except such as is common to man; but God is faithful, who will not allow you to be tempted beyond what you are able, but with the temptation will also make the way of escape that you may be able to bear it" (NIV). When sin tries to isolate me and make me feel ashamed, let me find comfort in your promise. Let me find hope in the fact that other people are struggling, and you have given us all a way out. Your strength will help us to overcome, and we do not need to be afraid of falling.

That might just be the most powerful knowledge there is when it comes to overcoming my temptations. God, you have promised that you will not let me be tempted beyond my ability to overcome it and will make a way of escape. Help me start looking for those escape routes, those secret doors, Father. Help me see those ways I can overcome when I am tempted. You really do have my back on this. I do not have to give in to temptation. You have overcome and I too can overcome! What an enlightening revelation.

You tell us to be strong and courageous. You tell us to follow the Ten Commandments. You tell us that in you, we can endure all manners of trials and temptations. I once feared temptation because I was sure it would lead me to sinning. Now I know, Lord, that temptations do not have to be my downfall. In your strength, I can overcome and be the person that you have called me to be. I need not be ashamed of my physical weakness, but find comfort in your strength.

I know, Lord, that you will always protect me. You will always keep my feet from stumbling. I need only trust you.

Amen.

12

DECEMBER - PERSEVERANCE

WEEK 1

$\mathcal{D}$ear God,

You have called me to endure hardships as a good soldier. Yet, I know that in order to be a good soldier, I am going to have to go through a lot of training. I am weak in flesh and in mind. Though I strive to grow closer to you every day, I do not always get it right. Help me to go through the necessary training to become the warrior you are calling me to be.

In the past, I have treated my trials as if they were the end of the road or some kind of punishment. It did not occur to me that they could be shaping me into a stronger, more resilient Christian. Sometimes, I blamed you for my trials and questioned why you would let me go through such a difficult situation. I grew frustrated when you did not answer my prayers the way I was hoping. I grew anxious when I had to wait for your response.

Forgive me for my pride and arrogance, O Lord. In the moment, everything was out of control, and I was not willing or able to see the good in the situation. My world was crashing down around me, and all I could think about was my own pain. Rather than crying out to you for help, I cursed your name. I blamed you for not protecting me better or preventing me from ending up in that situation. What I could not see at the time was you were protecting me from something even worse. Through my trial, you were preventing an even greater heartache.

What I know, Lord, is that you are good. That is your nature. So you did not cause the trials in my life. The sin in the world and the lies from the enemy are what cause these terrible things to happen. You do not desire to see your children in pain, but sometimes you do allow us to experience difficulties to help us grow closer to you.

That is my earnest desire, Lord. I want to endure my hardships as a good soldier so that I can grow closer to you. Help me to be grateful when trials come because they are increasing my faith and proving your goodness once again. Train me as your soldier, and teach me your ways.

Amen.

WEEK 2

Dear God,

When I wanted to increase my faith, I asked you to increase my trials. I wanted my faith to be tested so that it could grow even stronger. I ask the same now so that I may learn to persevere. In the past, trials and temptations have caused me to give up immediately. Even the most inconsequential obstacles made me want to throw in the towel. I have been weak in spirit and in the flesh. Rather than turning to you for help, I simply decided that perseverance was not worth the effort, and I would just do whatever I wanted.

However, Lord, I know that I cannot grow into the person you want me to be unless my perseverance grows. Just as I asked you to give me doubt to increase my faith and to give me extra burdens so that my strength may increase. I have learned that there is no way for me to get closer to you and to grow stronger in you unless I am willing to take on more. Sometimes the "more" will be good things. You will give me more love, and you will provide more peace. Other times, though, the more will be difficult. I will endure more trials, more temptations, and more pain.

In all of the "more," I want to glorify your name. If more heartbreak comes, may I turn to you for comfort. If more hatred comes, may I turn to you to receive love and to show that love to my enemies. When more temptation comes, please give me more grace to overcome it. When I look back over those instances and see how I responded, let me not have pride in how I handled those situations but in how you blessed me. May I boast of your presence in my life and deny that I had anything to do with it.

Increase my endurance, Lord, that I may persevere toward the finish line. Life is going to bring more difficulties and struggles, but I will keep my eyes on you. The world will continue to be out of control and unpredictable. Natural disasters will continue to devastate populations. Diseases and pandemics will continue to bring death and anxiety. Political unrest will cause more tension and division in the hearts of man. In all these things, I will stand firm on your promises. I will not fear the future and I will not give up on my faith out of that fear. I will not turn to anything else to bring my comfort, I will only derive comfort from your Spirit.

All you want from me is to keep going. You are asking me to keep one foot in front of the other and walk toward you. Send me obstacles so that when I fall, I will learn how to get back up. Send me pain so that when I am hurt, I will learn to turn to you for healing. Send me pressure so that when I am anxious, I will turn to you for rest. Send me fear so that I will turn to you for confidence. When I stop striving and growing closer to you, send me hardships to turn me back to your face. I never want to give up on following you.

Amen.

WEEK 3

Dear God,

Your strength is perfect when my strength is gone. When I have been at the end of my rope, you have always been there to give me more. Too many times I relied on myself when you were urging me to let go and trust that you would catch me. Rather than increasing in perseverance, I have increased in laziness. I have allowed my petty squabbles or small physical aches to keep me from following you. Rather than relying on your strength, I have relied on my own, but I see how that keeps me from persevering when I should.

God, you have proven to me in this last year that you are faithful and trustworthy. You have shown me so much of your character, and our relationship has gotten even closer. In the future, I would like to rely on you more because I know that in relying on you, I will be more likely to keep going. I will not worry about where my feet may walk as long as I am walking in your path. When people curse me or spit at me, I will rejoice that you have increased my circle of influence.

It is easy to grow discouraged, anxious, or fearful of the world. The enemy does not want me to succeed in your promises, and the world does not want to hear your Word. They will set up innumerable obstacles and trials to keep me from succeeding in my message. They will try to use political correctness to tell me that my beliefs are wrong or oppressive. They will put laws in place that disparage my beliefs and opinions. In every situation, they will be combative and angry. They will shout obscenities at me and make me feel like I am evil because I follow you.

I consider in those moments how Jesus must have felt when He was walking the Via Dolorosa to Calvary. The crowds were shouting at Him and cursing Him. They mocked Him, beat Him, tortured Him, and laughed at Him while He suffered. His body was so physically weak and His spirit must have felt crushed, but He still made that walk. He could have given up His spirit before making it to the place where they would hang Him. He could have asked you to intercede and make the suffering stop, which is what His dissenters kept yelling at him to do. He kept walking though, even when it was nearly impossible for Him to do so. He persevered all the way to the cross because He was so focused on saving us from our sin.

During this Advent season, I think of the baby who was born to die, and I am reminded that I can do all things through Christ. Even if I were asked to suffer and die for the salvation of others, to literally pick up my cross and follow Him to death, I would do it. I would surrender my will and my desires to glorify Him in all things.

You are worth it, Lord. Suffering for your sake is worth any pain or trials that I will endure in the future. I know that through your strength, I will be able to persevere through every circumstance.

Amen.

WEEK 4

Dear God,

This week we are preparing our hearts to celebrate Christmas. What a beautiful time of year to reflect on your promises and receive comfort. I have so many thoughts as the day draws near.

Firstly, I think of Mary. She was a young woman in a culture that did not value her. She had her role to play and rules to follow, but when you gave her Jesus, she had to break those rules. You broke those rules. There were probably so many people who did not believe her and wanted to punish her for getting pregnant out of wedlock. They probably wanted to put her to death or have her fiancé banish her and ruin her reputation forever.

Mary could have said "no" when you gave her the task of carrying your child. She could have said that she was not willing to go through the trials and hardships that she would face. She did not want to make her new husband doubt her, she did not want to bring shame to her family, and she did not want to flee for her life with her husband and new child when a king would try to murder them. Most of us would have said "no." She said "yes," though. We do not know what was going through her mind at the time, but we read that she was filled with joy and she was at peace.

I then think of Joseph. He also had to deal with the cultural shame of Mary's decision. Either people would think that they had a baby before they were wed, or they would think him weak for maintaining the honor of a woman who "cheated" on him. He would have experienced similar hardships as Mary, but he did not have the same encounter as she did. He did not agree to let his body be used to carry the Son of God.

Yet, when you sent your angel Gabriel to speak to him, he stayed faithful to Mary. He wed her as he had promised, and he fled with her into Egypt. He took care of his family, including the child that was not his, and he had to accept the fact that he was merely an earthly stand-in. When I think of Mary and Joseph, I can only think of their perseverance in faith. They said "yes" in all the times they could have said "no," and they followed your commands even when it was at great personal cost.

Then, I think about our culture and how we have turned Christmas into a selfish holiday. Sure, maybe you never intended for us to celebrate the birth of your Son, but instead we took His birthday and made it about ourselves. We give gifts to one another and let those gifts determine the level of love we feel. We spend at least a month stressing ourselves out and telling children the story of a man who is not you and who only brings them gifts if they behave.

There are so many thoughts and feelings I could unpack, but I simply ask this. Help me to change the way I celebrate the birth of your Son. Help me to lead my family in the worship and meditation of your gift. If we exchange gifts, let us be grateful for whatever we have received. If we go out to serve meals to those less fortunate, or sing worship hymns to shut-ins, let us do so with grateful and cheerful hearts. Let us make the birth of your Son a day to reflect on how much we love you, and see how we could love you even more.

Amen.

WEEK 5

Dear God,

What excites me most about following you is knowing that you will exist from everlasting to everlasting. There is no other god, no other being, no entity that has been and will be around for all of eternity. I know that I can persevere because you will always be there to uplift me.

This last year, as I have gotten closer to you and meditated on your Word, I have faced many challenges. The enemy has seen me draw closer to your presence and he did not like it. He wanted to keep me from you, to make me doubt who you are and what you can do for me. At every turn, he was there to attack me and weaken my resolve.

It did not work, though, because my hope, love, joy, and faith are all in you. There is nothing that he can do to me to make me doubt you. There are no obstacles he can put in my path that will make me turn around. I am committed to staying in your will, and I will persevere through whatever traps he tries to set for me.

A verse that has been repeated several times in the last year has been Isaiah 40:31. I have clung to that verse to bring me peace and keep me going. "Those who hope in the Lord will renew their strength. They will soar on wings like eagles; they will run and not grow weary, they will walk and not be faint" (Isaiah 40:31, NIV). What an encouragement it is to hope in you. What a restorative experience. If I hope in anyone else, if I believe in anyone else, I will run out of steam. Because I follow you, I will be granted the perseverance and endurance to keep going.

Lord, I know that trials are still going to come. It would be naive and reckless to believe that a relationship with you would wipe away any challenge in this life. In fact, the opposite is usually the case. We are promised difficulties and pain in this life, but even so we know that you are present and faithful. With everything that I have learned from you this year, I know that I can trust you to keep me going in the worst of times.

Father, when struggles come, may they bring me closer to you instead of pulling me further away. May I rest on your promises, then get back up and do work for your kingdom. When I run to tell your good news, do not let me grow weary. When I am speaking your hope and promises into others, do not let my voice become hoarse or for sickness to enter my body. If I am afflicted during these times, though, help me to spread your good news anyway. Help me to work in spite of any physical pain because I want to bring you glory.

When I am feeling discouraged and downtrodden, remind me that you are always with me, even to the end of the age. When I am anxious or afraid, put your peace and joy inside of my heart. God, I do not know what the next year is going to contain, but I know that as long as I take courage from you and choose to persevere, there is nothing I will not be able to do.

Amen.

If you enjoyed the God's Spiritual Warrior'sPrayer Handbook. I would deeply appreciate a REVIEW. This will help get the book out to many more believers, Thank you.

A SPECIAL GIFT TO THE READER !!

Included with your purchase of this book is our God's Spiritual Warriors Checklist.

In this checklist you will receive the 5 steps necessary to prepare for being a Spiritual Warriors. It will fortify you with the right tools, environment, and other techniques needed to get the most benefit out of your Handbooks.

Click below and let us know which email to deliver to.

drrockyspencer.com

REFERENCES

New International Version (NIV) Bible. (2016). Christian Media Bibles.

Wheeler, E., Rogers, W.B., Wheeler, M. A. M., Wheeler, W., Scriven, J.M. & Converse,

C.C. (1915). What a friend we have in Jesus.

https://www.loc.gov/item/jukebox-15866/.